THE PRIVATE EQUITY
DIGITAL OPERATING PARTNER

THE PRIVATE EQUITY DIGITAL OPERATING PARTNER

USING DIGITAL TRANSFORMATION FOR VALUE CREATION

Bruce Sinclair

Founder of digitaloperatingpartners.com

EVE ALLAN

Library of Congress Control Number: 2020922848

Copyright © 2021 by Bruce Sinclair.

All rights reserved.

No part of this book may be reproduced or transmitted in any form or by any means, electronic or mechanical, including photocopying, recording, or by any other information storage and retrieval system, without written permission.

ISBN 978-0-578-79953-7

Printed in the United States of America
10 9 8 7 6 5 4 3 2 1

To my wife, Jessica, and my children, Paris and Chase.

CONTENTS

Acknowledgments ix

INTRODUCTION
What's the Deal with Digital? xi

PART ONE
Valuable Digital Transformation

CHAPTER 1
Driving Value with Digital 3

CHAPTER 2
Best Practices 15

CHAPTER 3
Digital Transformation by the Numbers 25

CHAPTER 4
Technology Timing and Impact 39

PART TWO
Finding the Right Transformation Target

CHAPTER 5
The LBO Competitive Advantage 53

CHAPTER 6
The Most Suitable Portfolio Companies 63

PART THREE
The Digital Operating Partner

CHAPTER 7
The Role 75

CHAPTER 8
The Qualifications 85

CONCLUSION
Bring It On! 93

Index 101

ACKNOWLEDGMENTS

No one can be told what The Matrix is. You'll have to see it for yourself.

—*Morpheus*

Before our second child was born I confided to a friend and work colleague Brian that I didn't know how my wife and I were going to handle another child since we were still overwhelmed by how much our lives had changed after our first. To assuage my concerns, he said, "Bruce, the first child is a miracle and the second is logistics." Not exactly, but from a certain perspective he was right. This also applies to books. The miracle isn't gone but having written my first book, *IoT Inc.*, it made writing this one that much easier because I had already journeyed down the path.

This book was started and finished during the frontend of the COVID-19 pandemic. My simplified and monotonous day-to-day routine certainly made the task of writing easier. I'm always looking for the silver lining, so my first thanks is to the lockdown for making this book easier to complete.

Kidding aside, I'd first like to thank my previous private equity firm who recruited me to join their value creation team as an operating partner, the other partners I worked with and our portfolio companies who I spent most of my time with. This book is a direct result of that experience shaping my previous experience in the field.

I'd like to thank Shivanand Sawant and Daryl Moon, two of the best reviewers of my first book, who spent time reviewing this one.

And as before, I'm most grateful to my family. To my wife Jessica, who has always been supportive, and my children Paris and Chase, now away at University, who encouraged me from afar.

INTRODUCTION

WHAT'S THE DEAL WITH DIGITAL?

It's inevitable. It's coming. It's already here. All companies will become digital companies. I don't mean all companies will use digital (technology), because they already do. And I don't mean all companies will have internal tech projects under way or even a digital product, because many already do. I mean, given time, all companies will become data driven, using data to improve their physical operations and, more importantly, using customer data to improve every aspect of their products' customer experience. Given time, technology as a standalone sector will disappear as it permeates all other sectors.

If you're like most people, your first experience with a smart product came in 2007. At the time, I was living in Montreal and was the CEO of a networking company. We were developing a smart building platform but didn't have a good way to control it. We wanted a mobile solution, so we bought all the top-of-the-line phones to test, including the reigning Nokia N82. The browsing experience for all of them was terrible. Then, on a business trip to New York

City, I bought the iPhone 1. It wasn't yet available in Canada, so I had to have it "cracked" to make it work on our networks. I must say, it was a thing of beauty. Whereas the N82 was a phone with computing and networking capabilities, the iPhone was a computing and networking device with phone capabilities.

The iPhone was the first *smart* phone and, for many of us, the first smart product we ever saw or owned. Think back to the first time you used your iPhone or competing smartphone. Remember how it was better in almost every way than the traditional phone you used before it, and the feeling you had when you used it. That's the difference between a smart product and a traditional product, and that's the opportunity we have in front of us today for every kind of traditional product. Smart is so much better.

Even though we already have smart watches, smart speakers, smart homes and smart cars, this is just the beginning. Eventually all companies will sell smart products and have smart operations. Though that future is a little ways off, we are now witnessing the emergence of the *smart megatrend* that we can capitalize on as private equity (PE) investors.

Some companies are born digital, but for the rest the opportunity is in making them digital.

Smart companies outperform the broader market, independent of sector. All the reasons that make private equity successful as an asset class are the same reasons that make it best suited to digitally transform companies.

Transforming a traditional company into a digital-traditional company is a clear example of where the active management ethos of PE can do a better job than the average company left to its own devices. The desire for change, quick decision making and the rapid alignment of resources and incentives are hallmarks of private equity and what's exactly needed during digital transformation. Successful private equity firms actively support their portfolio companies to be bold and make big value moves while minimizing risk—to play to win, rather than to play not to lose. Successful private equity firms can realize the full potential of select investments by augmenting their current operational improvement playbook with digital transformation as a value creation tool.

DIGITAL TRANSFORMATION

What is digital transformation? Let's break it down. The *digital* part is described consistently across the board: Digital is technology. However, to put a finer point on it, digital, in PE, should be high technology such as the internet of things (IoT) and artificial intelligence (AI), not, for example, IT (low tech) or automation (mid tech). The differential value has been squeezed out of these older classes of technology resulting in their commoditization, and for those looking for an angle, commodity rarely results in differential advantage.

The *transformation* part of digital transformation is a little trickier to nail down, because if you believe search results, *every* application of tech is transformational. Of course it is, to SEO marketers, but for investors, not so much. So it's best to put digital transformation into context. In this book,

INTRODUCTION

The Private Equity Digital Operating Partner: Using Digital Transformation for Value Creation, the context is clear: Digital transformation for us is a value creation tool to increase the enterprise value of select portfolio companies by increasing their EBITDA and valuation multiple. For us, digital transformation is the transformation of a traditional company into a digital-traditional company by implementing one or more digital initiatives.

Digital transformation doesn't need to be complicated, but it does need to be strategic. Most companies will have a few digital initiatives cooking or maybe even baked, but most will fail because they're being developed for the wrong reasons and managed by the wrong people. The raison d'être for digital transformation, at least for us, is to produce data-driven companies. A data-driven company can become more valuable by using the same digital value creation playbooks as Amazon, Apple, Alphabet, Facebook and Microsoft, who create value with digital-enabled business models and digital intangible assets.

So what is digital transformation? It's a new source of alpha for private equity.

WHO IS THE DIGITAL OPERATING PARTNER?

The digital operating partner is the newest member of the value creation ops team. The tools of their trade are high technology, and they produce a new source of alpha by guiding their portfolio companies through a transformation that makes them data driven, enabling them to leverage the smart megatrend.

WHO IS THIS BOOK FOR?

This book is for general partners (GPs), limited partners (LPs), portfolio company executives and all the intermediaries who have a stake in company valuations. Ultimately, though, it is for investors—GPs looking to realize the full potential of their investments. This book explains digital transformation, the digital operating partner that implements it and the types of portfolio companies that can most benefit. It's for buyout firms open to expanding their worldview to find edge.

My first book, *IoT Inc*, was a business book about the internet of things—the foundation upon which every digital transformation is built. It taught managers and executives in every sector how to use high tech to create value and monetize that value with different business models, and it taught the strategic implications digital transformation will have for every industry. This book is an application of *IoT Inc* for private equity based on my experience as a PE operating partner. Compared with *IoT Inc*, this book is specific and brief rather than general and expansive, and it's written for the investor rather than the businessperson.

WHY YOU NEED TO READ THIS BOOK

Digital Transformation Is Coming to All Nontech Sectors

Digital is transforming the companies and products in all nontech industry sectors. We're witnessing this first as consumers, in our pockets, on our bodies and in our homes. Smart speakers like Amazon Echo and Google Home are now in a quarter of U.S. households, and almost 20 percent of all homes have a second smart product. Smart cars, usually referred to as self-driving or autonomous vehicles, have been digitally transformed to be data driven—the definition of a smart product.

This is just the beginning in B2C and the very beginning in B2B, with the smart megatrend washing over all traditional sectors, leaving behind new winners and losers in its wake. The winning companies will either lead or dominate their industries and will have been converted into data-driven companies—becoming part software and data science companies. Think about your portfolio companies. That's where the opportunity lies. Read this book to be able to identify your digital winners.

There's a New Way to Increase Enterprise Value

Digital transformation is a new value creation tool that enables your firm to capitalize on the smart megatrend leading to asset-light businesses in any sector. As a value lever, it's long in capabilities. Not only can it reduce COGS and

OPEX to improve margins; it is a platform for innovation that is primed to increase sales either by increasing market share through increased competitiveness or by entering new markets through disintermediation or other novel strategies. It can also ratchet up the valuation multiple. The quantification of value from being data driven can produce a product so competitive, like the iPhone, or a business model so compelling, like Uber's, that data-driven companies can dominate or even disrupt their industry. Hyperbole aside, it certainly doesn't need to be that dramatic to make a meaningful impact. The digital rerate, as you will learn, can justify a valuation multiple closer to the valuation multiple range assigned to tech companies with the uplift characterized as goodwill. When thought about strategically, an investment in the technology of digital transformation is an allocation of resources for growth—spurred by innovation and invention.

Digital Will Give Your Firm a Competitive Edge

Aggregate returns will continue to be of primary interest to investors, but how a GP creates value is increasingly important to LPs and GPs alike. Operational value creation has become private equity's primary source of value creation and really the only dependable source of value. Digital transformation furthers that reality and is a value creation lever that creates alpha independent of any other operational improvement mechanism, making it accretive to any firm's existing efforts. Doubling down on operational value creation will only make your firm more competitive and more likely to deliver top-quartile returns. The edge is yours by growing your ops team with a digital operating partner.

The Takeaway

After reading this book, you will understand digital transformation as a value creation tool. You will be able to identify prime company candidates for digital transformation by assessing your portfolio and reading CIMs with a new eye. And after reading this book, you will be able to find and hire the right digital operating partner by understanding what the digital operating partner does and what qualifications they need.

TERMINOLOGY

Before we get started, it's worth clarifying a couple of the often-used terms to avoid confusion. The first is *product*. In this book, the term *product* is overloaded to mean a product, or a service or an environment. Keep in mind that almost anything sold or used can be made "smart."

And although we'll discuss this in more detail, the *digital operating partner* (the second term) is also an overloaded term. Sure, it can be an individual operating partner who is an internal hire, but it can also be an external consultant or an internal or external digital team.

OVERVIEW

This book is about how the digital operating partner and their extended team, identifies, plans and executes valuable digital initiatives to transform traditional companies into data-driven companies that produce more innovative products, business models and operations.

The book is organized into three parts. Part One defines digital transformation: what it is, how it is applied and why it is used in the first place. Part Two of the book helps you understand the inherent advantages that buyout-owned companies have in digital transformation and what to actively manage during the transformation. Plus, this part helps you pattern match companies ideally suited for digital transformation. Part Three discusses the digital operating partner's role, responsibilities and qualifications, enabling you to make, if you're so inclined, an informed hiring decision.

Let's look at each of the three parts in more detail.

Part One

Part One answers all the questions—what, how, why and when—about digital transformation from the perspective of value creation within private equity.

It starts by comparing and contrasting traditional non-tech companies with digital/tech companies. Specifically, we isolate the key reason tech companies are so much more valuable than traditional companies, and within this context, we explain what digital transformation is, along with giving examples to illustrate the benefits of being digital. That's the "what."

Then we get into the heart of the book, value creation, and explain the three primary ways to use the high technology of digital transformation to create value. We also explain how digital transformation can "juice" our traditional portfolio companies with the same "superpowers" as their digital counterparts have. That's the "how."

Next we show the way we account for our newly created alpha by going to the financials to show the places digital transformation increases enterprise value by increasing its two multiplication factors: EBITDA and the valuation multiple. To demonstrate we further break down the ways to improve sales and reduce costs. Then we go through the digital rerate that lifts up the valuation multiple closer to the multiples assigned to tech companies. This is the "why."

We finish our discussion on digital transformation by breaking technology down into low tech, mid tech and high tech and analyzing when each class of technology is used for maximum impact. This is the "when."

Part Two

Part Two describes the first phase of digital transformation diligence to apply to your target or existing portfolio companies to decide if a more detailed and time-consuming next phase of diligence is necessary.

It starts by considering how employee behaviors resulting from different company ownership structures play into digital transformation success. The winning ownership structure becomes a foregone conclusion, but more important are the hot spots that need to be managed as the portfolio company goes through its digital transformation. After this we consider the non-ownership structure selection traits indicative of transformation success.

The companies that pass through these diligence phases are ready to enter value diligence, where they are qualified and quantified for their digital alpha creation potential.

Part Three

Part Three helps identify the right person or right team to perform digital transformation by tracing an outline around the ideal candidate. We start by defining this value creation role and describing how it's the same, and yet different from other operating partner roles.

We discuss how the job of the digital operating partner is different by describing the job's three major roles: the investment role of identifying companies and their digital initiatives that will have the highest digital return, the strategic business role of planning how to make the digital transformation a success and the execution role of ensuring the accurate and timely execution of the digital initiatives that make up the company's digital transformation plan.

Next, we dig into the qualifications needed by this individual or firm. We start with the digital operating partner's business qualifications, go through the candidate's education qualifications and finish with what the candidate needs to successfully execute the job—to put it all together and get it done.

* * *

Ready to begin? The book gets us started by describing how digital transformation provides traditional portfolio companies with the competitive advantages that come naturally to digital/tech companies. Let's go!

PART ONE

VALUABLE DIGITAL TRANSFORMATION

What is digital transformation? At its most basic, it's technology for change. IT is the tech that first comes to mind for many private investment professionals, but IT barely registers on our radar when considering digital value creation. For private equity (PE), digital should be synonymous with high technology such as the internet of things (IoT) and artificial intelligence (AI), because only high tech can deliver a meaningful impact on enterprise value.

As a value lever, digital transformation has it all. Like other operational improvement techniques, it can reduce costs and improve sales, but what's different is that digital transformation produces a structural change in the business that galvanizes innovation and invention. This is transformative because it also transforms the perception of the asset and its growth profile, contributing to an increase in the paid valuation multiple at exit. After reading Part One you will have a clear understanding of digital transformation from the perspective of operational and strategic value creation in private equity.

1

CHAPTER 1

DRIVING VALUE WITH DIGITAL

It isn't by accident that the most valuable companies in history are today's digital companies. When you think "innovation," the engine of growth, your first thoughts aren't traditional automobile manufacturers, taxicab companies and bookstores. Instead you think Tesla, Uber and Amazon—companies that use digital to create great products, great services and great business models.

These data-driven companies disrupted their industries and invented new ones, and in the process, they became the most valuable companies in their industries, and in history. Until recently, digital companies were synonymous with tech companies, but high technology now makes it practical to digitize the offline products and services of traditional companies to bring them online. This process is called *digital transformation*, and it enriches traditional companies with many of the same advantages previously enjoyed only by tech companies. The digital operating partner on the PE operations team identifies, plans and executes digital initiatives to produce meaningful revenue growth, improved margins and expanded multiples.

TRADITIONAL COMPANIES

First, let's start with some definitions. For our purposes traditional companies are companies like traditional auto companies, taxicab companies and bookstores. They sell nondigital products or services used offline in the physical world. Traditional companies create value offline and predominantly operate offline too. Traditional products are manufactured in atoms by scientists, engineers and tradespeople and are not connected to the traditional company's business (systems) after being sold. Industrials and manufacturing immediately come to mind as traditional company sectors, but due to the physicality of the definition, applicable sectors also include aerospace, healthcare, infrastructure, energy and natural resources. The traditional company is usually mature, but it can also be a younger company that just hasn't digitized yet, such as those companies in biotech and retail. In other words, traditional companies are most companies, and that's a good thing, because it means digital value creation is applicable to most of the companies in a buyout firm's portfolio. (See Figure 1.1.)

Figure 1.1	Traditional Company Attributes

- Example companies: GM, Yellow Cab, Barnes & Noble bookstore
- Sell physical products
- Products create value offline in physical world
- Products manufactured mainly in atoms
- Products not connected to customer after sale
- Candidates for digital transformation

DIGITAL COMPANIES

Digital companies are tech companies like Tesla, Uber and Amazon. Technology is their product, and it's usually represented as a platform or an app. These companies were born digital and sell products and services that create value online and predominantly manage operations online too (Figure 1.2). Digital products are manufactured in bits by programmers, hardware designers and data scientists and are tethered to their digital company's business (systems) after being sold. And while they may also employ atoms to operate in the physical world, from a value perspective, the atoms are simply a vessel to be operated by software and driven by data. Digital companies are not good candidates for digital transformation because they are already digital and data driven. These companies include but are not limited to those that operate within purely tech sectors such as software, telecom and, well, the technology sector.

> **Figure 1.2 | Digital/Tech Company Attributes**
>
> - Example companies: Tesla, Uber, Amazon
> - Sell digital products
> - Products create value online
> - Products manufactured mainly in bits
> - Products connected to customer after sale
> - Not candidates for digital transformation

DIGITAL VERSUS TRADITIONAL

Besides being used in the digital world versus the physical world, and besides consisting of bits (software) instead of atoms, the most profound difference between digital and traditional companies is that digital companies are data-driven companies. Digital companies are connected to their customers 24 hours a day, 7 days a week, with a high-bandwidth network connection between the customer/user and the digital company. It is through this customer-product-company business system connection that companies get to know their customer. They know how the customer uses their products (usability), they know what the customer uses their products for (utility), and perhaps most importantly, they know how their customer makes money from using their products. Customer data is one of the intangible assets that's made digital companies the most valuable companies. Value that's created by innovating their products and inventing new ones. Value that's created by innovating their business models and inventing new ones. This same data can also be used to increase margins through operational efficiency, but most of the value comes from growing the top line with amazing products and dominating industries with amazing business models, all of which lead to insurmountable advantages over their traditional competition.

Sounds like hyperbole, but that's exactly what Tesla, Uber and Amazon are doing today along with thousands of other well-run digital companies. Let's compare Tesla with, say, GM. While the list is long, I'll just focus on a few areas of product and business model innovation and invention that differentiate Tesla.

- **Autopilot:** Tesla's autonomous vehicle software differs from competitive systems like GM's Cruise in the way it builds its self-driving models. Rather than building them from the ground up, Tesla merges its customers' driving behaviors and reactions with sensor fusion to iteratively improve its autonomous driving.

- **Smart Summon:** Like a robotic valet, Summon will park your Tesla after you've arrived at your destination, and then it will unpark it to pick you up from your current location when you're ready to leave.

- **Direct:** Tesla has no distributors. It has disintermediated the traditional automotive distribution channel by selling direct to the customer to improve margins and control aftermarket sales.

- **Insurance:** Tesla will soon sell auto insurance. Who knows the driver better than the driver's own car? This enables Tesla to sell a new product priced to be profitable for any driver. This is what I call outcome integration, which in many cases is more valuable than vertical or horizontal integration and, in this case, will disrupt the automotive insurance industry.

And did I mention Tesla also plans to invert the current auto revenue model by enabling owners to make money with their cars? By opting into Tesla's Robotaxi fleet, your car can make you money instead of waiting for you in its parking space.

All these innovations are made possible because of the direct connection Tesla has with its customers. In contrast, GM's connection with its customers is practically severed after the sale. And since GM doesn't "own" the customer, GM must rely on its channel to provide it with customer data. Because gathering customer data indirectly is such an onerous and time-consuming task, the amount of data collected is limited and, by nature, biased.

Digital innovation and invention are at the core of Tesla's success. That's why when Tesla's share price crossed $1,000, it surpassed Toyota to be the most valuable automobile company in the world. Worth more than double GM and Ford combined, all the while producing one-tenth the number of vehicles. Auto manufacturing isn't alone. In sector after sector, smart products, services and environments are disrupting the incumbents and the markets they sell to. But there is a way to compete with this: digital transformation. It's being used in every sector, and now that it's out of the research lab, it's available to GPs to be their newest value creation tool.

DIGITAL TRANSFORMATION

Digital transformation is the process of transforming a traditional company into a digital-traditional company (Figure 1.3). The process is the sum of one or more digital initiatives, or projects, that are chosen based on the company-specific alpha they can produce and the cost of the resources to do so. This is the hard part. Not the technology; that's relatively straightforward when working with the right teams. The hard part is identifying the right initiatives to implement and then costing them out. This is the job of the digital operating partner—to identify, plan and execute these digital projects. Some will produce short-term wins and others will be longer-term in nature, but when summed together, they can make a meaningful difference in enterprise value within the hold period of an investment.

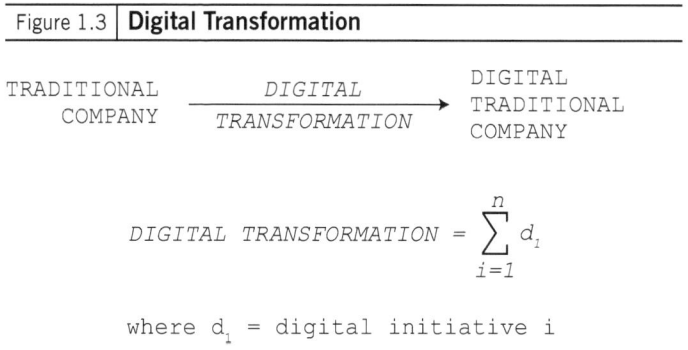

Figure 1.3 | Digital Transformation

TRADITIONAL COMPANY → *DIGITAL TRANSFORMATION* → DIGITAL TRADITIONAL COMPANY

$$DIGITAL\ TRANSFORMATION = \sum_{i=1}^{n} d_i$$

where d_i = digital initiative i

These digital projects require tech. The technology chosen is typically based on the maturity of the portfolio company: for early-stage companies, low tech such as IT and business systems (BI, CRM, PLM, ERP) make a big difference. Similarly, for mid-stage companies, the tech is usually of the automation, RPA, digital marketing and ecommerce variety. But low tech and mid tech have been commoditized and produce commensurate results; they're necessary for a well-running business, but they're usually table stakes priced into the deal. The highest-impact tech for value creation is high technology, especially when applied to mature companies.

High tech is no longer limited to venture capital. Since the risk profile of implementing digital transformation technologies has dropped with usage, high tech is now being exploited by LBOs as their newest enterprise value creation tool. Although it's a moving target, current high tech that has been sufficiently derisked includes the internet of things for gathering data, and also data science (analytics and AI/machine learning [ML]) to interpret the collected data to create value. These are the two foundational technologies that make digital-traditional companies digital. Other key high tech includes the digital twin, sensor fusion, additive manufacturing, augmented reality (AR) and, to a lesser extent, blockchain. Put together, the sweet spot of digital transformation is the use of high technology to make legacy/traditional companies data driven. For a more detailed discussion on low, mid and high technology, read Chapter 4.

DIGITAL-TRADITIONAL COMPANIES

Digital transformation makes a data-driven company from a traditional company, and the underlying purpose of the data and the drive is simple but powerful: to better understand the customer. This is the digitally transformed company, what we refer to as the *digital-traditional company*: a traditional company that operates online in the physical world. A traditional company that, like Tesla, has a direct connection to its customers via its smart physical product, service or environment. But it doesn't end with innovative smart products and business models; a digital-traditional company can also use its primary customer data to improve sales and marketing as well as maintenance and support. In fact, the data collected by the digital-traditional company can potentially produce competitive advantages in all its operating departments. Privacy issues aside, interpreting customer data improves the customer experience and increases competitiveness, which in turn increases enterprise value. (See Figure 1.4.)

Figure 1.4	Company Comparison		
	TRADITIONAL COMPANY	DIGITAL COMPANY	DIGITAL-TRADITIONAL COMPANY
CREATE VALUE:	Offline	Online + sometimes offline	Online + offline
PRODUCTS MADE OF:	Mainly atoms	Mainly bits	Bits + atoms
CONNECTED TO CUSTOMER:	No	Yes	Yes
DATA DRIVEN:	No	Yes	Yes

THE BENEFITS OF BEING DIGITAL

At a high level, the benefits of being data driven like Tesla, Uber, Amazon and other digital and digital-traditional companies originate from collecting and using customer data, allowing the companies to make better products and sell them within better business models—a win-win for all.

Value created by digital transformation improves cash flow and the valuation multiple.

Sales are increased by digital initiatives that make the product better, increasing market share; and other initiatives use customer data to invent new products, increasing market size. Cash flow is further improved by reducing COGS and OPEX by digital initiatives focused on asset utilization, capacity, production yield and quality.

The valuation multiple is improved by leveraging the structural changes made to support digital into a narrative of increased growth and derisked future cash flows. More specifically, in addition to supporting the nontech themes of the investment thesis, there is also what I call the digital rerate, articulated in the digital investment thesis. A digital rerate is achieved by deploying new business models and by replicating other novel strategies from the tech company's playbook. A digital rerate also creates digital goodwill. Goodwill that strategics will account for on their balance sheet after the trade sale by valuing the digital structural changes made by the digital-traditional company as being transferable to the strategic's organization to use as the template or starting point for its own digital transformation.

Let's pause here to differentiate digital transformation as a value creator from other operational value creation tools. Most value creation tools used today improve margins, which obviously has an impact, in fact often more of an impact than financial engineering. But the potential impact of top-line and multiple growth from digital transformation is greater.

The digital-traditional company gets the best of both worlds: It continues to create value with its physical products, and it amplifies that value and uses it in different ways by digitizing it—thereby impacting its customer, its industry and of course its valuation.

DATA DRIVEN TO ALPHA

The competitive advantages that come naturally to digital companies are now attainable by traditional companies, big and small, which become digital by incorporating high technology within their products and companies.

Digital transformation produces a data-driven company. A company that is more valuable because it uses the customer data it collects to improve sales, customer satisfaction and operations. Market size and market share are increased by using the data to fuel innovation and invention. Customer satisfaction is improved by providing a better customer experience. And the data is internalized to make company operations more efficient and customer centric.

Digital transformation creates alpha by ratcheting up the portfolio company's valuation multiple and improving its cash flow through sales growth and margin expansion. It is a new and powerful operational value creation tool that complements the value creation toolbox of any buyout firm.

• • •

We are getting to know the "what." What digital transformation is, what digital-traditional companies are and what the benefits of being digital are. Now let's dive deeper to understand the "how." In Chapter 2 we examine *how* private equity can apply the high technology of digital transformation to increase the enterprise value of its portfolio companies.

CHAPTER 2

BEST PRACTICES

We live in the age of the technology hype cycle. It's almost deafening as each high tech takes its turn cresting in hype until its successor takes its place. The storyline is always the same: First the tech is worshiped, then its powers are described as if they were science fiction and finally some of the tech applications prove themselves to be practical and capable of creating value and sometimes disruption.

Just as private equity looks for long-term trends within the noise of market cycles to find tailwinds for its investments, there is an opportunity to do the same with tech: to look through the noise of the hype cycles for long-term trends to provide similar investment advantages. Venture capital does it by making bets before the tech has proved itself. That's not the role of LBOs. Instead they have the luxury of time to wait for the tech to derisk before using it to create value and sometimes disruption.

This is the job of the PE digital operating partner: to use these proven high technologies like IoT and AI as tools by pattern-matching winning tech applications within the portfolio companies. The process of applying these high technologies to create value is called *digital transformation*, and now it is an important source of alpha that's been either overlooked or deemed too complicated until now.

With financial engineering hardly moving the needle and traditional operating improvements becoming commoditized, it's worth it for private equity to consider how the best practices for digital transformation can produce value in the PE's fund.

As discussed, digital transformation is the process of transforming a traditional company into a digital-traditional company through a series of digital initiatives that create value by using high technology like the internet of things, data science (analytics and AI/ML), the digital twin, sensor fusion, additive manufacturing, AR and blockchain. Digital transformation transforms traditional companies into data-driven companies (Figure 2.1), providing a platform for product innovation/invention, business model innovation/invention and greater operating efficiency, all leading to the North Star of increased enterprise value through EBITDA and valuation multiple gains.

| Figure 2.1 | **Transformation to Data Driven** |

PRODUCT INNOVATION

Collecting customer data with a smart product (or smart service or smart environment) is like having a 24-hour-a-day, 7-day-a-week window into the customer's world. From this data, different data science models are built to yield different business insights.

Usability models quantify how customers use their smart product, and just like an ecommerce company uses its usability model to improve its website, a digital-traditional company uses its usability model to make its physical smart product better too.

Take, for example, the road roller, aka the steam roller. Road rollers use their weight of up to 44,000 pounds and their vibrating drum to remove air from the hot mixed asphalt (HMA) to compress it to a specific density. Getting it right takes a lot of experience, and even then, it can be hit and miss. Enter digital transformation. Every geography has a known ideal asphalt density to make the perfect road. By digitizing the variables associated with asphalt density (HMA temperature, roller weight, roller speed and drum vibration frequency), we can build a paving usability model and then solve it in several different ways. To minimize time (increase efficiency) while achieving the desired asphalt density, we solve for max speed and control the speed of the smart road roller accordingly. (See Figure 2.2.) To minimize material usage (reduce COGS) while achieving the desired asphalt density, we solve for HMA thickness.

| Figure 2.2 | Usability Model |

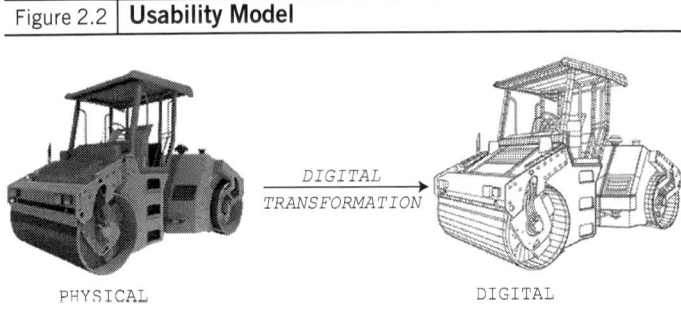

PHYSICAL   DIGITAL

```
Roller Speed = f (asphalt density, HMA thickness, HMA temp,
     roller weight, drum vibration frequency)
```

Which product is more valuable? A regular road roller that's operated by gut or a smart road roller that compresses asphalt to the perfect density under different circumstances in any environment. Usability models like this are a platform to catalyze countless innovations. Innovations that lead to a more competitive product that produces alpha by increasing market share, which leads to higher sales and higher EBITDA.

PRODUCT INVENTION

A utility model tells us what the customer uses our product for, and when properly developed, empowers us to invent new products, both physical and virtual.

Consider a smart surgical instrument–cleaning autoclave. In this example a simple utility model is used to measure machine capacity, what is being cleaned and how well it cleans. If over time we discover the trend that our smart surgical autoclave is being disproportionately used to clean a specific type of long surgical instrument, we have potentially discovered a need for a new product—one that matches the long instrument's geometry, cleaning capacity needs and best cleaning mechanism. Furthermore, we can sell this new physical product along with custom-cleaning consumables formulated to clean the instruments in the new product. And by knowing how the autoclave is being used, we could sell an information product that tracks sustainability, or we could underwrite a product warrantee that is always profitable. We can invent new products by quantifying how our original product was being used. (See Figure 2.3.)

Figure 2.3 | **Utility Model and Its New Products**

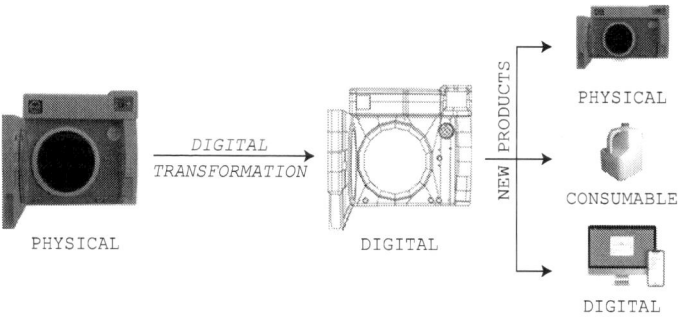

Utility = f (instrument size, cleaning volume, type of cleaning mechanism)

Another class of model that produces valuable information products is prediction models. These models use past and present data to make predictions about the future. A use case for prediction that's applicable to both the smart road roller and the smart surgical autoclave is maintenance. Prediction models can be taught to understand normal operating conditions and quantify multidimensional conditions that eventually lead to failure. These predictions can lead to two types of new information products: a predictive maintenance product that notifies the operator of impending doom and a prescriptive maintenance product that makes changes to the smart product's configuration to avoid or delay the failure before it happens.

Inventing new physical products and tailor-made consumables and information products all expand market size and find alpha by shifting the boundaries of competition or by entering adjacent markets. This too increases sales and EBITDA in a meaningful way.

BUSINESS MODEL INNOVATION AND INVENTION

Another class of data science model to consider is monetizability models. These models understand how the customer makes money with your product. Modeling the variables of your customer's revenue model leads to two profound and related operating improvements: product pricing and product monetization.

Pricing improvement/rationalization is a go-to value creation lever used in private equity today; however, it is performed with experience, gut instinct and data. A pricing digital initiative driven by a monetizability model is all about the data. If we can measure the amount of revenue or profit generated by our product, we can value price it with extreme precision.

Pricing on its own increases sales, but as part of a custom-built business model it can also disrupt industries. Once we quantify the business model of our customer in relation to our product, we can transpose it to create a new business model that interfaces with the customer's business model to reduce sales friction.

Digital transformation supports a number of classes of new business and revenue models, one of which is XaaS (anything as a service). A simple example comes from the aviation sector where jet engines are sold as a service. The most important KPI of the airline industry is miles flown per occupied seat—a metric that influences, among other things, airline share price and management compensation. A term originally coined by Bristol Siddeley and then popularized by Rolls Royce and GE, the "power by the hour" business model charges airlines based on the time the engine is used. This business model disrupted the airline industry by relating costs to revenue and shifting the capital expenditure off the airlines' balance sheet.

Not only can new business models increase sales to improve EBITDA, they can also affect the valuation multiple. Changing the business model or introducing other novel digital strategies is a thick chapter in the playbooks of the most valuable and, not surprisingly, most innovative tech companies. Automotive, music, video, housing . . . time and time again tech companies have disrupted legacy industries by structurally changing the business or customer experience based on customer data. Through digital transformation, this is now available to PE's traditional portfolio companies that sell physical products.

OPERATIONAL EFFICIENCY IMPROVEMENTS

Until now, we've been looking at the external benefits of digital transformation: benefits that have improved the customer experience and company competitiveness. Next, we turn our view internally to see how digital can reduce our operating costs and expenses. Cost cutting is a common application of digital transformation. Not because it's more valuable, but because until now cutting costs is what naturally comes to mind when most corporates and GPs think about information technology. Nonetheless, digital transformation can improve operational efficiency by improving asset utilization (people and equipment), production yield, availability, capacity, performance and quality. Let's look at a few examples to see how.

Logistics can improve supply chain visibility by using track & trace technology to feed real-time data into models that, once developed, can be optimized for time (speeding up delivery) or for any other KPI, such as reducing fuel consumption. Biotech, after digitizing the "pots and pans" of by-hand experimentation, can use data science to identify the experiments to do that have the highest probability of success.

In these examples, alpha is organically created, but digital transformation can also support inorganic growth. Buy and build and TAM expansion acquisition strategies can be supported by extending the tech into the add-ons to integrate them into the platform company. Not integration in the sense of plumbing, but instead integrating the data being carried by the IT pipes. One such example is to use data science to predict overall platform and add-on inventory needs for working capital improvement, supply chain rationalization and group buying power.

Operational efficiency lowers COGS, and by using the customer data collected by the smart product, it can improve SG&A effectiveness too. This reduction of COGS and OPEX widens margins, increasing enterprise value by improving EBITDA.

THE NEWEST VALUE CREATION TOOL

Digitally transforming a traditional company into a digital-traditional company produces a data-driven company. Once the physical has been digitized, portfolio companies can take advantage of the same value creation strategies used by the most valuable tech companies. Data-driven companies build models such as usability models, utility models, prediction models, monetizability models and optimization models that in turn galvanize product innovation, product invention, business model innovation/invention and operating efficiency.

Digital transformation and its associated high technologies have been derisked so they can now deliver an important source of alpha additive to the other operational improvements typically applied by private equity operation teams. As a value generator, not only does digital improve margins, but it enables a variety of ways to increase the top line and valuation multiple, making digital one of the most powerful operational value creation tools available to GPs today.

• • •

How we create value with digital transformation is central to the role of the digital operating partner. There are many ways of reducing costs with high tech, but there are even more ways to increase the top line. In Chapter 3 we account for *why* digital transformation improves EBITDA and the valuation multiple in a portfolio company's financials.

CHAPTER 3

DIGITAL TRANSFORMATION BY THE NUMBERS

Digital transformation has been in the technical press for years; geeking out on everything from the merits of low-level network protocol design to high-level platform architecture. That's all good for a nerd like me, but now that the technology of digital transformation has matured, it's time to discuss it from a financial perspective—in particular, from the financial perspective of the leveraged buyout firm. Why? Because it's a perfect fit for GP portfolio companies, and it's now ready to be put to work by the digital operating partner as their primary value creation tool.

There are as many definitions of digital transformation as there are different interests in it, but from our perspective, the perspective of maximizing enterprise value, digital transformation is the transformation of a traditional company into a digital-traditional company through one or more digital initiatives. Digital enables us to operationally transform most types of portfolio companies into the type of companies that have the highest valuations: tech companies. For example, there are traditional companies like taxicab companies that operate in the physical world and digital companies like Uber that operate in both the virtual and physical worlds. Both roughly do the same thing, but the one that is more valuable is obvious.

Most operational improvements in private equity deal in percentages. Percentage of costs, percentage of working capital and percentage of price, which yield fractional improvements. Digital transformation can hit harder with whole-number improvements in EBITDA and the valuation multiple. Next, we'll break down enterprise value to see how fund managers can create alpha by using this new operational value creation tool. Time to geek out financially.

ENTERPRISE VALUE

```
ENTERPRISE VALUE = EBITDA x
      VALUATION MULTIPLE
```

As a value driver, digital transformation has it all. Not only does it employ digital initiatives to turn down COGS and OPEX, but it can also turn up the two biggest knobs of enterprise value: revenue growth and the valuation multiple. Data-driven operational improvements increase cash flow and provide different options to ratchet up the valuation multiple during the holding period. Enterprise value is our North Star. We always go back to EBITDA and valuation multiple when choosing which digital initiatives to implement when designing a portfolio company's digital transformation.

EBITDA

```
EBITDA = net income + interest +
taxes + depreciation + amortization
```

Let's focus on cash first. Examining EBITDA is a great way to isolate the portfolio company's profitability from its core operations before considering the impact of capital structure, leverage and other non–cash flow items. To do this we will look at net income's revenue and then margin.

```
Net income = revenue - COGS - OPEX
+/- other profit/(loss) line items
```

REVENUE

When considering operational improvements as measured by EBITDA gains, the X factor is revenue growth. Revenue solves all problems. Whether from inorganic growth or price rationalization, it's all good, but the most coveted growth comes from increasing market share and market size—both being the sweet spots of digital transformation because they're both the sweet spots of digital companies. (See Figure 3.1.)

When we think about the most successful companies as measured by valuation/enterprise value, digital companies such as Microsoft, Apple and Alphabet come to mind. In fact, tech companies, including these, are the most valuable companies in history. Digital transformation enables traditional portfolio companies to have the "superpowers" of tech companies, and the common denominator of the most valuable tech companies is that they are all data driven. So the source of these superpowers is data—data to help you understand how customers use your products (usability), what they use your products for (utility) and how they make money with your products (monetizability). Networking tech and software give digital companies a direct connection to their customers through their smart products. This primary customer data drives successful organizations to make better products (innovation) and make new products (invention), but it's not limited there: it also enables these data-driven companies to innovate their business models and even invent new ones.

This is the "why" of digital transformation. To transform traditional portfolio companies into digital-traditional portfolio companies is to make them more data driven, because traditional companies that are data driven (digital-traditional companies) can use the same playbooks as the ones that made Microsoft, Apple, Alphabet and other tech companies so valuable.

MARKET SHARE

All things being equal, market share goes to the company with the most competitive product. For successful digital companies this alpha comes from interpreting customer data to improve usability and utility. In the same way Apple observed its iTunes software users to improve its interface, functionality and performance and then produced iTunes' successor Apple Music, smart tractors from John Deere have been similarly improved through usability and utility. John Deere's smart products are the most innovative in the company's industry and as a result enjoy the greatest market share.

MARKET SIZE

Alpha from increasing market size is achieved by entering new markets. Data-driven companies minimize the risk of entering new markets by using customer data to invent new products or innovate existing products to serve their new markets.

Microsoft used 15 years of customer data gathered from Windows to inform the design and function of its then new Xbox game console, launching the company into a growing $35 billion market. Fast-forward 20 years, and game revenue represents almost 10 percent ($11.4 billion) of its total revenue. The Xbox console differentiated itself by being not only smart but also connected (networked like a PC), allowing customers to play each other, not just play against the game software. From game hardware Microsoft grew into producing game software and now uses the microtransactions business model for in-game purchases.

In the physical world, Continental Tire used its smart tires to invent new information products for the fleet management market. Today Continental sells a new information product into a new market to monitor safety and logistics costs, and in the process, the tire company has increased the size of its total addressable market.

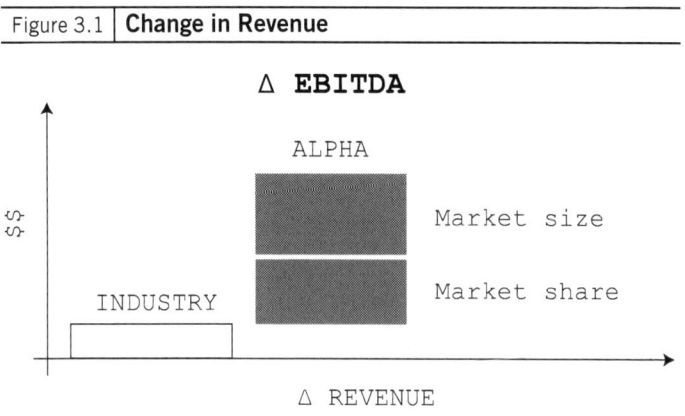

Figure 3.1 | Change in Revenue

PROFIT MARGIN

In general, margin expansion with digital transformation is about using data science to reduce costs and expenses through operational efficiency. Analytics and AI/ML is used to interpret data from the portfolio company's operations sensors to improve one or more of asset utilization, human capital utilization, production yield, availability, capacity, performance and quality.

While digital can support traditional expense reduction efforts such as salesforce efficiencies, inventory management, group buying power, and supply chain and distribution efficiency, its main focus is to measure and optimize the operations of creating a product or providing a service. Operations are quantified and then efficiency/

performance models are developed, improved and interrogated to provide useful information to improve profit margin. (See Figure 3.2.)

COGS

Robots and other automation devices have been reducing the cost of goods sold for decades. Digital transformation goes one step further by creating a layer above this equipment and other assets to orchestrate them. This is the purpose of the industrial internet of things (IIoT) and Industrie 4.0 (I40): to digitize and stitch together devices and a plethora of high technology to deliver digital initiatives such as predictive maintenance, asset monitoring, asset tracking and fleet management. To support these initiatives, capital is redirected to high technology to create a digital twin of the portfolio company's manufacturing or production processes.

This is digital transformation as it pertains to the production of products, but the customer data collected can also reduce operating expenses by improving the efficiency of other functional departments within the organization.

OPEX

Understanding how your customers use your product/service, why they use your product and how they make money using your product produces data that can be used to improve virtually every department in the digital-traditional company. For example, product usability data can be used to optimize SG&A spending by knowing or predicting when there are opportunities to sell more products or product consumables. Similarly, product utility data can be used to create marketing communications customized for each customer.

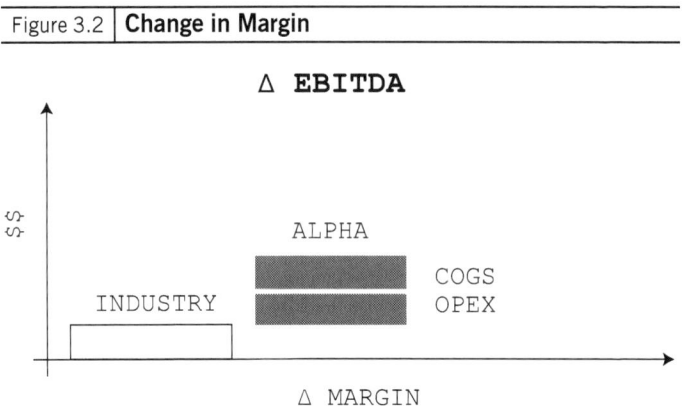

Figure 3.2 | Change in Margin

VALUATION MULTIPLE

In addition to taking advantage of arbitrage, negotiation skills and market inefficiencies, the job of the buyout firm at exit is to convince the buyer that the asset for sale is well positioned for future growth and profitability—to substantiate its premium valuation multiple.

The structural changes from being digital can be a strong company-specific component of the narrative used to communicate an increase in the growth profile and a decrease in the risk profile of future cash flows. Digital helps accomplish this in two ways: the support of nondigital investment thesis strategies and the digital rerate.

INVESTMENT THESIS SUPPORT

Part of the digital investment thesis is to support and amplify the strategies in the overall investment thesis to increase the asset's growth profile (Figure 3.3). Inorganic strategies such as buy and build and TAM expansion (horizontal or vertical or geographic integration) are supported by extending digital capabilities into the add-ons to integrate them with the platform. This is not the plumbing integration of IT but the integration of the data within the overall data science strategy focused on improving the platform company's KPIs. Another step is to digitally integrate the platform and add-on companies' products.

Figure 3.3	Investment Thesis Support

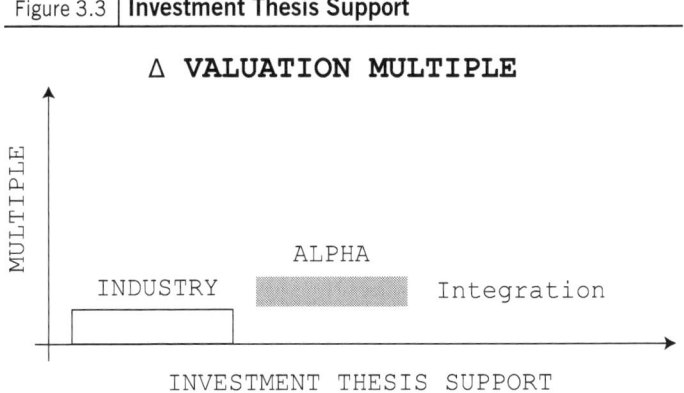

DIGITAL RERATE

The digital rerate takes three forms: valuation migration, premium goodwill and potential disruption.

Valuation Migration

The first form of a digital rerate is the step-by-step migration of the valuation multiple from the purchase multiple up to a multiple closer to the valuation multiple of digital/tech companies (Figure 3.4). This is based on the perception that the traditional company has become more like a tech company—e.g., after a theoretical 100 percent digital transformation, the traditional portfolio company would be a digital company and therefore command a tech valuation multiple. Since no digital transformation is fully completed during a hold period, a partial digital transformation will garner a partial tech valuation. And being unfinished is not

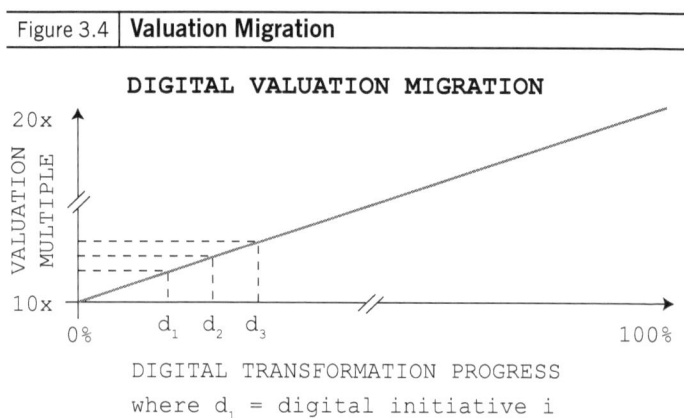

Figure 3.4 | Valuation Migration

bad news. On the contrary, it is an opportunity for further value creation, so it represents a credible future growth narrative that can be sold as upside to the next buyer.

Premium Goodwill

The second form of digital rerate centers on digital goodwill (Figure 3.5): goodwill that a strategic buyer will pay for to justify the inflated valuation multiple. Digital transformation is hard, and it's even harder to do in a corporate structure where there are multiple shareholders. It's not that the technology is any harder; it's not. It's harder because of all the nontech reasons, the same reasons why multishareholder companies don't generally perform as well as PE-owned companies: strategy and alignment. Because digital transformation is hard to get off the ground for strategics, they will highly value the architecture of a smart product/platform and the assembly of a digital team and use them both as the starting point or to augment their own digital transformation. Strategics will account for this intangible asset on their balance sheet as goodwill after the acquisition, and the number can be quite large.

Potential Disruption

The third form of digital rerate derives from deploying innovative business models and other novel strategies supported by digital. This is an elusive but common trait of the most successful digital companies. Of course, digital does not guarantee the disruption of competitors and industries, but it does represent the home run of value creation (Figure 3.5).

Examples of innovative business models in the digital space include Apple's pay per song in iTunes and its all-you-can-eat subscription model in Apple Music, Microsoft's microtransactions in its video games and Alphabet's pay per click and pay per conversion in Google Ads. Disruption requires innovative and inventive products, but these awesome products are usually accompanied by awesome, or shall we say, innovative and inventive business models.

These strategies disrupted the music industry, the electronic games industry and the advertising industry. Data from the customer-product-company connection enabled each disruption, and as such, all three strategies can be deployed by legacy companies too.

A digitally transformed company has this same type of data coming from its physical products. GE sells its jet engines by the hour because its physical products are digitized. John Deere sells outcomes from its tractors and only shares in profits because its physical products are digitized. Same thing for Tesla. Because its physical products are digitized, Tesla is expanding its TAM by starting to sell auto insurance. By knowing how its customers drive, Tesla can underwrite policies that will always be highly competitive and profitable. And coming up, Tesla will offer to buy unused vehicle capacity from its customers. Soon Tesla owners will be able to make money from their car when it's not in use by opting into Tesla's upcoming Robotaxi services. That's disruptive and reproducible by other digital-traditional companies, but novel strategies like these don't need to disrupt industries to drastically increase the slope of the digital-traditional company's growth profile.

Digital transformation supports innovation and invention that, in turn, supports a steeper growth profile—a growth trend that is sustainable because going digital is a structural change, not a short-term blip in cash flow.

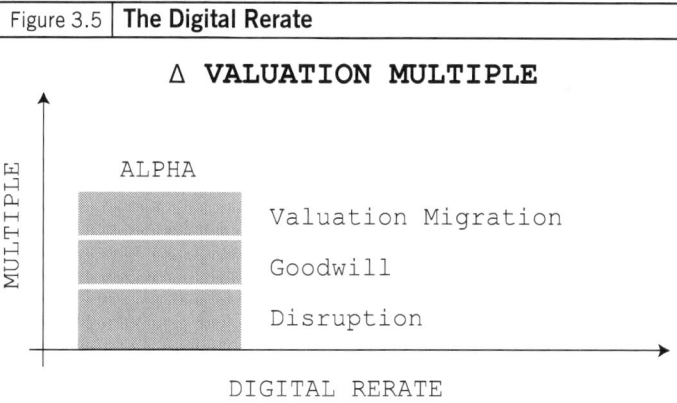

Figure 3.5 | The Digital Rerate

THE DIGITAL PAYOFF

Now that the high technology of digital transformation has matured out of venture, it can be used by buyout firms to help produce superior returns for its investors. As a value lever, it creates alpha EBITDA growth and an alpha uplift in the portfolio company's valuation multiple (Figure 3.6).

Figure 3.6 | **Alpha Created with Digital**

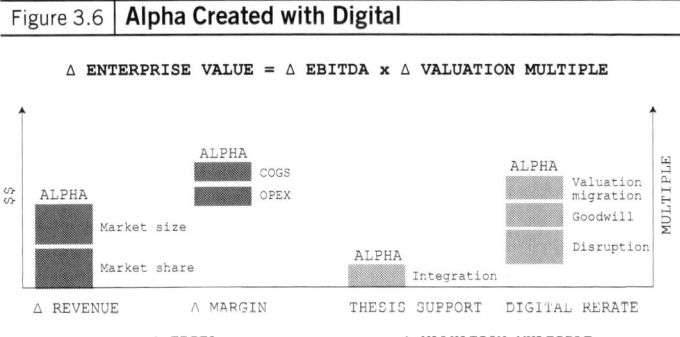

Digital transformation splices digital company genes into the DNA of traditional portfolio companies, and the resulting data-driven "superpowers" express themselves in value after the portfolio company crosses the digital divide.

• • •

Digital transformation compounds enterprise value by increasing both of its multiplication factors: EBITDA and the valuation multiple. Next, we shift from finance to technology by reviewing the digital operating partner's tools of the trade. In Chapter 4 we differentiate the three levels of tech available to private equity and discuss when they are applied and why digital transformation uses high technology for maximum impact.

CHAPTER 4

TECHNOLOGY TIMING AND IMPACT

It's surprising that, in private equity, IT is almost synonymous with technology. Nothing could be further from the truth. There's a lot more that PE can do with tech than implement back-office infrastructure.

Digital transformation is the transformation of a traditional company into a digital-traditional company by implementing a series of digital initiatives. Digital means technology, but in this context it's important to distinguish the different types of technologies that companies can put to work and when these technologies have the most impact.

For our purposes, there are three levels of technology: low tech, mid tech and high tech (Figure 4.1). We will discuss what they are, how they create value and the best time to use them during the life cycle of the portfolio company. But mostly we will discuss the biggest moneymaker, digital transformation, and how the digital operating partner uses its high technologies to create value.

Figure 4.1 | Tech Classified by Impact

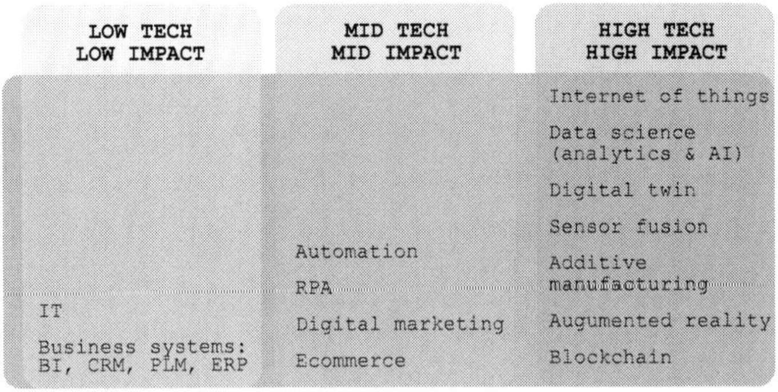

LOW TECH LOW IMPACT	MID TECH MID IMPACT	HIGH TECH HIGH IMPACT
		Internet of things
		Data science (analytics & AI)
		Digital twin
		Sensor fusion
	Automation	Additive manufacturing
IT	RPA	Augmented reality
Business systems: BI, CRM, PLM, ERP	Digital marketing	Blockchain
	Ecommerce	

We begin by defining the tech in each level.

LOW TECH

- **IT:** Information technology is the plumbing (networking) that connects compute devices (computers, phones) to each other, storage (local, network, cloud) and business systems. In digital transformation the IT and OT (operating technology) networks connect the equipment that makes the smart product or is the network in the smart product.

- **Business systems:** Each functional group has a business system to help with its operation. Examples include BI (business intelligence) for management, CRM for sales/marketing, PLM for manufacturing and ERP for operations. In digital transformation, business systems hold the data used and produced by smart products to create and improve data science models.

Low tech, as defined here, was considered high tech in the '80s, but since then it has faded into the background and is now in use by all companies. Infrastructure tech like this enables value creation, but it has been commoditized to the point that it rarely produces competitive advantage. Low tech is low impact when it comes to value creation for the buyout firm.

MID TECH

- **Automation:** Automation is used to replace repeatable human physical activities with mostly mechanical (e.g., robots, conveyers) and electronic (e.g., cameras) devices. These devices are controlled by simple software within a closed and proprietary network. In digital transformation the industrial internet of things or Industrie 4.0 is used to orchestrate these automated devices based on operating efficiency models and others.

- **Robotic process automation:** RPA is used to replace repeatable human keyboard actions with software (called bots) that control one or more app interfaces. It is usually used to automate back-office tasks, such as inputting an invoice, that were previously done manually. A digital transformation initiative could have the smart product tell the RPA to submit a support ticket based on a smart product event.

- **Digital marketing:** This is a process for automating repeatable demand generation tasks. It uses email, social, web, search, online advertising and other digital tools to fill and manage the sales and marketing funnel. An example is an automated email sequence designed to move the prospect down the funnel. A digital transformation initiative could gather customer data from the smart product to personalize marketing communications.

- **Ecommerce:** Electronic commerce automates the buying and selling of products/services over the internet. An example is the storefront on a corporate website. A digital transformation initiative could have the smart product automatically order and bill a customer when a new consumable, part or product is needed or predicted to be needed.

The common theme for this 20–30-year-old class of technology is automation. Automating physical activity, automating keyboard activity, automating marketing and automating sales. Automation improves enterprise value by increasing EBITDA by reducing COGS and OPEX. It is a form of operating efficiency that improves output, capacity and performance, yielding expanded margins. This is good, but margin expansion doesn't generally have the same impact on enterprise value as increasing sales or increasing the valuation model. Therefore, mid tech has a mid-level impact on value creation for the typical buyout firm.

HIGH TECH

- **IoT:** The internet of things is an extension of the internet into physical devices. It consists of the software-defined product (application and data science model of how the smart product creates value), the hardware-defined product (compute, storage and communications), network fabric (IT and OT networks [fog] and cloud) and external systems (external data sources and other smart products). The purpose of IoT is to digitize the physical world for data science to produce digital twins of the product's value creation mechanism. Digital transformation gathers and processes data from a smart product's sensors and external data to create, improve and execute data science models.

- **Data science:** Data science consists of two branches: analytics and AI, and is a superset of BI. Analytics is statistics, and AI today is machine learning, which is statistics wrapped in probabilistic learning algorithms. Both are wrapped in a software container to produce data science models. In digital transformation, data science ingests the data from IoT to create and improve models that can look into the past to make sense of what happened, understand what's happening in the present and look into the future to make predictions of what may happen. In the context of cognitive automation, it can be used to replace repeatable human perception activities such as looking for signs of defects as discrete or process products come out of production/manufacturing.

- **Digital twin:** A digital twin consists of a federation of data science models that together mathematically simulate a part, product or system. In digital transformation the digital twin describes how the product produces value. The digital twin's value models simulate physical, biological or chemical processes. For example, in Chapter 2, how the road roller compresses asphalt was simulated with a usability model. This model is part of the road roller's digital twin.

- **Sensor fusion:** One or more physical- or biological- or chemical-based sensors are chosen based on the data requirements of the digital twin. Sensors are placed near, on or in the smart product. In digital transformation they output product data into IoT's network fabric, which then transports it to computation that can live locally, in the fog (local network) or in the cloud.

- **Additive manufacturing:** AM, or 3D printing, is a new form of discrete manufacturing that physically reproduces 3D geometry models by depositing material in 2D layers. Advancements revolve around materials science. AM can reproduce most CAD models or can be driven by AI to reproduce unimaginable designs. A digital transformation initiative could be to use additive manufacturing as part of a mass customization solution.

- **Augmented reality:** AR visually combines the physical world with the digital world to provide insights not visible independently. This is not to be confused with VR (virtual reality), which only displays digital worlds. A digital transformation initiative can be to visually superimpose product data over the physical product when looking at it. This is useful for many operating tasks such as service for example, where a technician can overlay diagnostic or other information directly on the product being repaired.

- **Blockchain:** Blockchain is a decentralized immutable list of activities locked to an asset. The subtech of interest for digital transformation is the distributed ledger technology (DLT) that, for example, is used publicly in bitcoin. A digital transformation initiative can use blockchain to validate the history of all the actions involving a supply chain or ingredients or parts. This securely disintermediates the middleman to improve efficiency and reduce costs.

IoT, data science, the digital twin—these are today's highest technology and the fundamental tech used in today's digital transformations. This is the technology the digital operating partner uses to create the most alpha and the biggest increase in enterprise value.

When put together, high technology is used to make portfolio companies data driven—or to be more precise, customer data driven. By using the internet of things to transform traditional products into data-emitting products, and then data science to produce analytical and machine learning models from the data gathered, traditional companies can better understand their customers: how the customers use their products, what the customers use their products for and how the customers make money from using their products. This information is used to innovate existing products and to invent new ones, leading to higher sales and EBITDA by increasing market share and market size. But being customer driven also empowers traditional companies to innovate their business models and invent new ones, following the playbooks of the most successful tech companies. A "digital rerate" justifies a higher valuation multiple, one that's closer to those of tech companies than traditional companies. Of all the technologies available to LBO firms today, high tech has the highest impact on value creation.

WHICH TECH WHEN?

Low tech, mid tech, high tech. Any of these techs can be applied to create value at any company stage, but there is a natural progression to maximize that value (Figure 4.2).

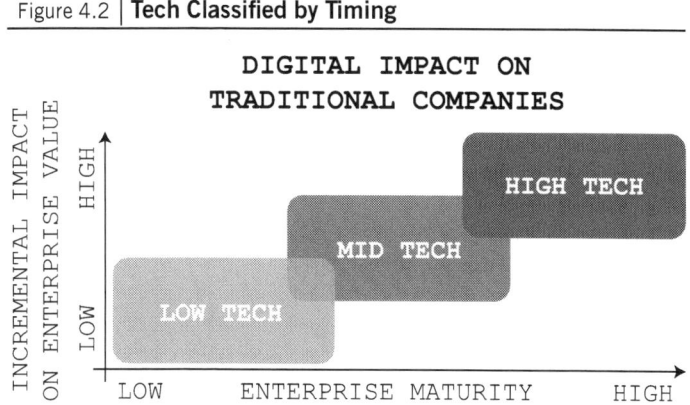

Figure 4.2 | Tech Classified by Timing

Early-stage companies, because they have likely incorporated high tech from the start, are not candidates for digital transformation, but if they are still doing accounting using QuickBooks, then low tech, in the form of business systems, is valuable. Therefore, low tech has the most impact on early-stage (venture-backed) companies.

Conversely, mid-stage companies, in all likelihood, already have enterprise-level IT and business systems in place, so for them, low tech provides little incremental enterprise value. But mid tech, with its ability to automate repetitive human activities, is valuable. It's rational to implement mid tech to gather the lowest-hanging fruit value before moving to the more specialized high technology. Implementing mid tech (and low tech) does not require unique talent. Mid technology is established enough to almost be plug and play, and there are plenty of resources, both internal and external, that have the needed implementation skills. Therefore, mid tech has the most impact on mid-stage companies, those older than early-stage companies and younger than mature companies. Mid-stage companies are most likely later-stage venture or growth capital companies.

Mature companies, specifically mature, nontech companies, have the most to gain from high technology. They are of a vintage before today's high tech was invented. They already have low tech in place and most likely mid tech too. Of course, there are exceptions to when low or mid tech will provide value to mature companies. For example, integrating the business systems of an add-on and replicating a business system (lift and shift) in a carveout can both be important to mature portfolio companies. However, overall, low tech and mid tech are not as valuable as high technology to the mature LBO portfolio company. Though high tech is second nature to younger companies, the strategic use of high technology is still relatively rare for mature companies, so this presents a big opportunity to their owners.

From another perspective, each technology class builds upon the previous generation of tech. The low tech, or what can be considered the operational layer, is the foundation upon which all other techs sit. Atop the operational layer is the mid tech, or automation layer, that creates independent value and improves the operational layer with efficiency. And currently sitting on top of the mid tech is today's high tech, or smart layer, that creates its own independent value and improves the automation layer with data-driven cognition. Each technology class builds upon the previous generation's technology to create the full digital stack (Figure 4.3).

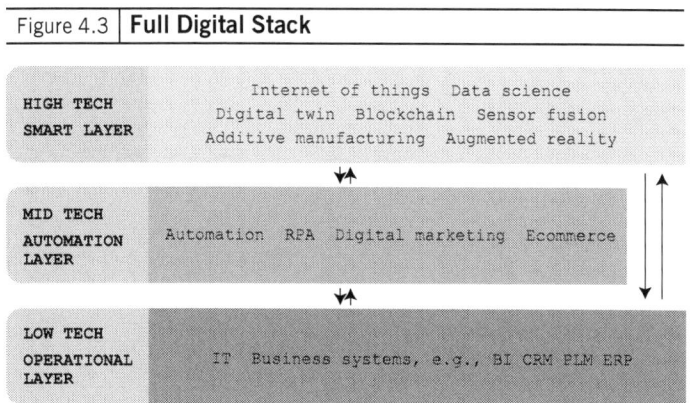

Figure 4.3 | Full Digital Stack

LIFE CYCLE IMPACT

For each stage in a company's life cycle, there is a class of technology that delivers the greatest impact to value creation. From the perspective of the mature company, low tech has a low impact, mid tech has mid-level impact and high tech has a high impact.

Digital transformation and its high technologies hold the most value for traditional, mature companies, like the ones found in many LBOs' portfolios today. When done properly, digital transformation widens margins, but more importantly, it also grows sales and grows the valuation multiple by borrowing from the digital innovation playbooks used by today's most valuable tech companies.

Because it's new and a good fit, digital transformation as an operational value creation tool presents an untapped opportunity for most buyout firms to further increase the worth of their portfolio companies.

. . .

Now that we understand what digital transformation is, why we do it and how and when to use it to create value, we move on to Part Two to find the right transformation target—one that has the traits indicative of digital transformation success.

PART TWO

FINDING THE RIGHT TRANSFORMATION TARGET

Every company is a snowflake. And because every company has different products, different competitors and therefore a different strategy, every company to be digitally transformed will have a different digital investment thesis leading to the design of a customized digital transformation. What isn't different, however, is the technology used. It's always the same. So, what makes for a successful digital transformation? It starts with the investment thesis of course, but there is another important success factor that's under our control: the portfolio companies we select to transform. Nontechnical factors such as the behaviors resulting from company ownership structure and other telltale traits are used as a screen during early diligence. In Part Two we discuss the inherent advantages an LBO-owned company has over other types of private and public companies, the behaviors that must be actively managed

51

and the other traits to look for in our portfolio companies that are indicative of digital transformation success. After reading Part Two, you will be able to identify existing companies in your portfolio that are candidates for digital transformation and companies in diligence that could also be contenders.

CHAPTER 5

THE LBO COMPETITIVE ADVANTAGE

Digital transformation is the operational transformation of a traditional company into a digital-traditional company. The digital operating partner uses high technology such as the internet of things and data science (analytics, AI/ML) to deliver digital initiatives designed to increase enterprise value.

Digital transformation is hard, but it's for reasons that may seem counterintuitive. Tech such as IoT and data science is on the cutting edge, so of course it's a challenge, but tech is a manageable challenge with the right experience and development partners. So it's not really the hardware or the software that presents the biggest undertaking; it's the wetware. As in any operational transformation, it's the human element that presents the biggest risk. However, experience has shown that when employees are in the right environment, this risk can be mitigated.

And that is the purpose of this chapter: to compare how the working environments imposed by different company ownership structures contribute to digital transformation success and to recognize the resulting behaviors to be managed during the transformation.

Assuming similar capital, people and physical resources, we will examine the effect that company ownership structure and the actions they promote have on digital transformation success. To do this we will compare the environments of public and private companies, then private strategics and sponsor-owned companies and finally VC-owned and buyout-owned portfolio companies, to identify the best ownership structure and behaviors for digital transformation to succeed.

PUBLIC VERSUS PRIVATE

First let's compare public company environments with private company environments as they pertain to supporting a successful digital transformation.

The most obvious place to start is governance. Having a multitude of public shareholders to answer to generally results in a more bureaucratic and hierarchical management structure than found in private companies. This structure is great for balancing many stakeholders' demands but less great for changing priorities and making timely decisions. Public boards are also more defensive in nature, more concerned with risk and not losing, rather than playing offensively to win. Successful digital transformation is more about effective leadership than effective management. Leadership that can make big decisions and then rally the troops to make them happen. The concentrated ownership of private companies ensures more effective decision making and the prioritization of strategies deemed to have the greatest value. With fewer institutional loyalties and distractions, the private company is better able to make dispassionate decisions and then have them carried out.

One of a public company's biggest distractions is quarterly reporting. The "end-of-the-quarter drill" can derail all business as usual, including, for example, diverting the digital team to help sales close those last few accounts before quarter end. Experience has shown it's best to establish a digital team, almost like a startup, that's insulated from public company gyrations so the team members can concentrate all their energy on implementing their digital mandate. This tends to be easier to do in private companies that can afford to have longer time horizons for their investments to pay off.

Defining a digital transformation strategy and creating an internal digital team to execute it implies top-down decisions. But in most public companies just the opposite occurs. Ideas for digital projects mostly come from engineering. Sometimes this can be great, but more often than not, engineering-driven digital initiatives are about the tech—the shiniest bells and the clearest whistles that are supercool technology but not so cool from an investment impact perspective. Experience has shown time and time again that without the right leadership and culture, digital initiatives will pop up in labs without business plans, consuming precious opportunity cost, only to be stillborn because the projects weren't valuable enough to raise the internal funds necessary to go commercial.

Although most discourse on digital transformation centers on public companies, it is the privately owned enterprises that have a better chance of digital transformation success (Figure 5.1).

```
PRIVATE > PUBLIC

A private company has a
better ownership structure
for digital transformation
than a public company.
```

CORPORATE VERSUS PORTFOLIO

Because private companies are better suited than public companies to digitally transform, let's break them down into non–sponsor-owned companies (corporates) and sponsor-owned portfolio companies.

Digital transformation, as the name implies, requires a transformational change in business operations. Portfolio companies have a built-in platform for change—change is the reason private equity made the investment in the first place. Without change there is no new alpha, and new alpha is the difference between a good exit and a top-quartile exit. Suffice it to say, private portfolio companies are meant to change, and if digital transformation is part of the investment thesis, then the impetus for digital change will come from the top down, through ownership, board and then management.

Experience has shown that without CEO and C-suite support, digital transformation will never see the light of commercialization. Private corporates with long-term CEOs and boards tend to have a lower sense of urgency and a "current-state" bias, preferring to stay the course and make incremental changes rather than transformational ones, even if those hard decisions are what's right for the company. If digital transformation is part of the investment thesis, private equity investors will ensure the current management team is ready and capable of making changes quickly, or adjustments will be made. Once the right team is in place, the compensation models will be structured to be tightly aligned with the value creation plans of ownership.

Portfolio companies are motivated, supported and incented to be bold and make big moves, giving them a better chance of digital transformation success than corporates (Figure 5.1).

```
PORTFOLIO > CORPORATE

A portfolio company has a
better ownership structure
for digital transformation
than a corporate company.
```

VENTURE VERSUS BUYOUT

Because private equity–owned portfolio companies are better suited than corporate private companies for digital transformation, let's zoom in to compare venture capital portfolio companies with LBO portfolio companies.

When comparing the two, it comes down to fit. Again, digital transformation is the operational transformation of a traditional company into a digital-traditional company. The best companies to transform are traditional, aka nontechnical companies. Furthermore, these companies are typically mature, because if they weren't, they would have started out digital in the first place. Older nontech companies don't fit the profile of a venture-backed company, but would be right at home in an LBO's fund.

Moving to digital is also a better fit for the operating model of the buyout firm—one that uses active ownership and an internal team of operating partners or external service providers to actively improve the operations of its companies. In this case active ownership means the digital team identifies the digital initiatives, plans them with the deal team and portfolio company's management and then implements them by hiring the right service providers, vendors and subject-matter experts from the digital operating partner's ecosystem.

The percentage of company ownership also plays a role. Unlike the buyout firm that has majority ownership, the venture firm doesn't generally own enough of the portfolio company to singlehandedly align management to a new digital strategy.

Portfolio composition and operating model make digital transformation a better fit for the buyout firm than the venture capital firm (Figure 5.1).

```
              BUYOUT > VENTURE

     A buyout portfolio company has a
       better ownership structure for
         digital transformation than a
     venture capital portfolio company.
```

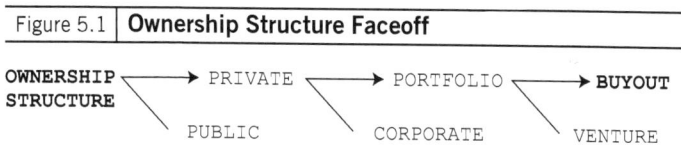

Figure 5.1 | Ownership Structure Faceoff

OWNERSHIP STRUCTURE AS A COMPETITIVE ADVANTAGE

The buyout portfolio company has the environment most conducive to digital transformation success—better than venture portfolio companies and strategics, private or public. This is a big deal. One that represents a significant competitive advantage for the company and its owners.

The natural evolution of all products is to go digital and become smart. Some industries will transform into digital industries before others. But make no mistake about it—all industries and the companies within them are becoming digital; it's just a matter of time.

If done properly, the first company to go digital will become or stay the dominant player in its industry. Therefore, the increased probability for digital transformation success represents a significant competitive advantage for the LBO portfolio company. It's an advantage that can be parlayed into industry dominance or even industry disruption.

The LBO firm with the appetite and ability to apply digital transformation within its portfolio companies also has a competitive advantage over other LBO firms. It is the inevitability of digital within all sectors that makes digitally transformed companies so attractive to strategics. Because of this, LBO firms with digital chops will, on the whole, have more attractive assets, which ultimately leads to better-performing funds. On the buy side, more targets are attractive because digital transformation is well suited to be applied to assets in the secondary buyout market. No matter how well run the company, further value can be created with digital transformation, assuming the right company attributes.

A PLATFORM FOR CHANGE

Digital transformation is a new and powerful tool to create enterprise value in portfolio companies. Since the technology used is the same for every company, all things being equal, it's the nontechnical factors such as the ability to rapidly make changes and align resources that make the difference in digital transformation success (Figure 5.2).

| Figure 5.2 | **Digital Transformation Success Factors** |

- A desire for change
- Quick decision making
- Rapid resource and incentive alignment
- Fewer distractions
- Value-added ownership

It's simple arithmetic. Having a platform for change, plus effective decision making, less distractions, plus a fit with the owner's operating model adds up to LBO portfolio companies having the best ownership structure for digital transformation.

Digital transformation is teed up to be private equity's next dominant enterprise value creation tool, one that will result in better returns and higher competitiveness for both the PE's portfolio companies and its fund. To do so the natural advantages afforded to the LBO company must be actively managed to maximize success.

* * *

Understanding the hot points to consider when coaching the CEO is instrumental in getting the culture right for transformation. Next, we look at the other traits used to filter our portfolio companies. Chapter 6 reveals the nonvalue-based traits used early during diligence to filter for the best digital transformation contenders.

CHAPTER 6

THE MOST SUITABLE PORTFOLIO COMPANIES

The most competitive companies of our age are digital companies. And the biggest of these digital/tech companies are being investigated for antitrust because they're regarded as being so competitive that they're repressing all their competition. Intrinsically related to this narrative is data. Facebook, Amazon and Google are said to know too much about us, their customers. This isn't by chance. There is a causal relationship between customer data and competitiveness: the more the company knows about its customers, the more competitive it is. Privacy issues aside, this is what we want for our portfolio companies. Not the antitrust thing—well, maybe the antitrust thing—but what we want more is for our companies to be so competitive that they dominate their markets.

Being data driven is the hallmark of all the most valuable and innovative companies today, and in history. Being data driven comes naturally to tech companies that sell digital products that are used online, create value online and predominantly operate online. Why? Because with software, customer data is easily accessible. This has put traditional competitors at a disadvantage. Amazon, Uber and Tesla have inherent competitive advantages over traditional bookstores, taxicab companies and traditional automotive manufacturers, but this hasn't been lost on these traditional competitors. To various levels of success, they are all transforming themselves into digital-traditional companies so they too can reap the rewards of using customer data as a competitive weapon. This is and will be the same story for all industries.

Digital transformation is the process of transforming a traditional company into a digital-traditional company. The digital operating partner uses high technology to transform traditional companies into companies that use data to drive initiatives that increase competitiveness. This increased competitiveness helps traditional companies increase sales, expand margins and, in many cases, ratchet up their valuation multiple by taking advantage of the structural changes resulting from the transformation. Put another way, data-driven companies are more valuable companies.

Here we look at the traits that best identify portfolio companies that have the highest potential from being digitally transformed and becoming data driven.

THE COMPETITIVE ADVANTAGES OF BEING DIGITAL

The competitive advantages of being digital, or of being data driven, enable digital-traditional companies to outperform their traditional competitors and, in some cases, to be so competitive that they disrupt their industries. Digital-traditional companies have a comparative advantage over their traditional rivals from using tech and data to increase operating efficiency, which improves their margins. Perhaps more important though, digital-traditional companies can use the customer data they collect to increase their differential advantage over their competitors.

The differential advantage of being data driven results in smart products that are unique and of higher quality than the products of their traditional competitors. Think Amazon versus traditional bookstores, Uber versus traditional cab companies, Tesla versus traditional automotive manufacturers and you get the picture. When done properly, smart products are better products as measured by usability, functionality and performance, and by almost every other metric, because they know what their customers need. Data-driven companies have a full-time window into their customers' worlds, and if the companies look, they can see how their customers use their products and what the customers use their products for. This leads to more innovative products that increase sales by earning more market share, and it leads to new products that increase sales by expanding market share (Figure 6.1).

Knowing how your customers make money, and how much money they make from using your product, leads to more rational pricing and to inventing new business models. New business models can lead to the hypercompetitiveness that dominates and even disrupts industries. Of course this is

> **Figure 6.1 | Data-Driven Competitive Advantages**
>
> COMPARATIVE ADVANTAGE
> - Increase operational efficiency with data science
>
> DIFFERENTIAL ADVANTAGE
> - Innovate and invent new products with data science
> - Innovate and invent new business models with data science

not guaranteed, but interfacing your business model to your customer's reduces monetization friction and in the process can have wide-ranging effects such as disintermediating the vulnerable, shifting the boundaries of competitiveness and subsuming conventional product categories, along with other novel and potentially disruptive strategies.

Because of the unique skills and company conditions necessary to create smart products, there is a high barrier to entry. And even if the digital functionality is duplicated, competitors can't duplicate the amount of data that was captured in the meantime. It is important to be first. Where a traditional product's value is in its physicality, the value of a smart product is derived not only from its physical characteristics but even more so from its software and data characteristics.

CANDIDATE COMPANY TRAITS

At a high level, one of the main components of digital transformation is the digitization of the value a company creates. The collected data is then transformed into useful information that is used to increase enterprise value. All this is independent of geography, the size of the company and, for the most part, the industry sector. With the exception of sectors like software, telecommunications or any other tech-heavy sector, digital transformation is broadly applicable to pretty much all other sectors, including aerospace, biotech/life sciences, consumer, energy, healthcare, industrials, infrastructure, manufacturing, natural resources, retail and transportation.

Although geography, company size and, for the most part, industry sectors are not significant, there are other traits that are and should be used to help identify the best candidate companies in a GP's portfolio to digitally transform. The sweet spot comprises companies that are traditional, more mature and not already in a market that has been digitally disrupted. It is these companies that have the most potential for an enterprise value uplift from digital transformation.

A TRADITIONAL COMPANY

The first trait to look for in potential digital transformation candidates is digitalization level. This translates into whether the company is considered traditional. Traditional companies sell nondigital products that are used offline in the physical world. Traditional companies create value offline, and although they may use digital products, they predominantly operate offline too. Traditional products are manufactured in atoms and are not connected to the traditional company's business (systems) after being sold.

Until recently tech companies were the only data-driven companies, but now high technology makes it practical to digitize the offline products of traditional companies to make them data driven too. Traditional companies are candidates for digital transformation because, by definition, they are not already digital, and so they have the most to gain.

A MATURE COMPANY

The second company trait to look for in your fund is maturity. Not maturity as measured in elapsed time, although there's a correlation, but technical maturity as measured in the technology that has so far been deployed within the enterprise.

From a value perspective there are three classes of technology. Low tech, which includes IT and business systems; mid tech, which includes automation, RPA, digital marketing and ecommerce; and high tech, which includes the internet of things, data science (analytics, AI/ML), the digital twin, additive manufacturing, AR and blockchain. It is high technology that digital transformation is made from.

There's a natural progression to deploying technology in traditional companies. In the early stages the company will deploy its tech infrastructure—its low tech. Later on, it will deploy mid tech/automation to improve operational efficiency. Today's mature company may have a high-tech initiative or two started (usually for the wrong reasons), but on the whole these companies generally don't have the DNA to deploy high technology in a meaningful way. Even though high tech is second nature to younger companies, the fundamental use of high technology is still relatively rare for mature/legacy companies because of their vintage, so this presents a new opportunity to their owners.

COMPANIES IN NONDISRUPTED MARKETS

One way to look at a market within a sector is whether or not it has been digitally disrupted yet, or less dramatically, whether or not there already exists a dominant digital competitor. Although fighting digital with better digital is certainly a rational strategy, it's an even better strategy to digitally transform a company in a market that doesn't yet have a real digital player.

As discussed, companies in most sectors can be improved by digital, but digital transformation is most valuable and most disruptive in markets where the competitive space still uses traditional products in the physical world. Another important trait to look for in portfolio companies relates to the markets in which they operate. Are companies operating in a market that hasn't changed much in years or even decades? Legacy markets that are less innovative are brimming with companies that are prime candidates for digital transformation.

THE IDEAL ASSET

Time has proved that digital companies become the most valuable companies in their market. There are those that are born digital (tech companies), and now there are those that have been transformed into digital. Both of these types of data-driven companies are the most competitive, capable of disrupting their markets and inventing new ones—and in the process, these companies become the most valuable in their market.

Identifying portfolio companies that are best suited for digital transformation is always the first phase of digital diligence (Figure 6.2). Ideal candidates are nondigital, nontech companies that are most likely to be traditional, mature companies operating in markets that haven't been digitally disrupted yet.

Figure 6.2 | **First Phase of Digital Diligence**

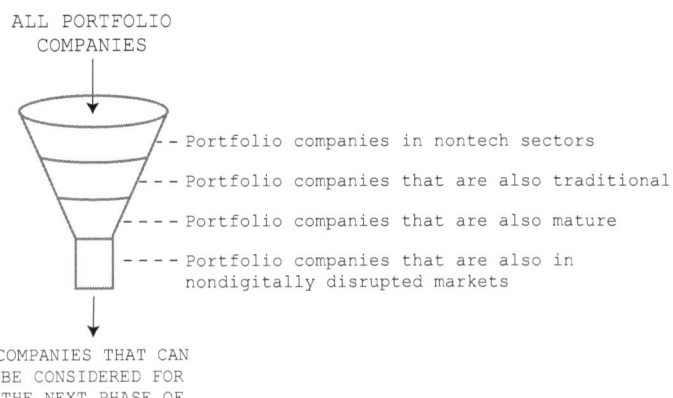

Private equity has a new value lever in digital transformation that once pulled will lift these companies up to the next valuation level.

* * *

There are three macro ingredients in digital transformation: The first two are the tech of digital transformation we covered in Part One, and the target portfolio company that we covered here in Part Two. The third ingredient is the talent. In Part Three we get to know the digital operating partner—the role of the person or team in charge of digital transformation for private equity.

PART THREE

THE DIGITAL OPERATING PARTNER

To use digital transformation as an operational value creation tool within your private equity firm, someone needs to be in charge, and that person is the digital operating partner. Part Three of this book is about providing the information you need to hire your own digital operating partner. Now, this doesn't necessarily need to be an in-house operating partner. In this book, *digital operating partner* is used as a general term for the internal or external person or team responsible for creating the digital investment thesis, creating the digital transformation plan to implement the thesis and then executing the plan to deliver the identified alpha, on spec, on time and on budget. Think of Part Three as a long job description or RFP, outlining the role, the responsibilities and the qualifications needed to capably digitally transform companies within your portfolio.

With this information you will be able to start your digital discussion with the appropriate subject-matter experts and service providers.

CHAPTER 7

THE ROLE

Meet the digital operating partner, the newest member of the private equity operating team. The digital operating partner is a senior business executive with an interdisciplinary background in business strategy, in science and technology and in hands-on operations. Like that of other operating partners, the role of digital operating partner is to increase the enterprise value of the PE firm's portfolio companies. But digital operating partners do it in a very different way. The tools of their trade are high technology, and their job is to use IoT and AI to transform select traditional companies in the portfolio, piece by piece, into digital-traditional companies. The newly data-driven companies will then use technology to further innovate and invent their products, their operations and their business models.

This operational transformation is called digital transformation, and it represents a new angle for private equity at a time when fund managers are facing their highest competition. It's a powerful angle that is new and produces a distinct source of alpha in an environment characterized by shorter financial levers, and less luck in arbitrage and discovering market inefficiencies.

ROLE

The enterprise value created by the digital operating partner hits the financials in three places. First, sales alpha is increased by using high tech to improve products, increasing market share, and to invent new products, increasing market size. Second, margin alpha is produced by using technical efficiencies to lower COGS and, to a lesser extent, OPEX, by improving asset utilization (people and equipment), production yield, capacity and performance. Together they raise EBITDA, which is always a good thing. And third, technology, when used in the way the most valuable tech companies use technology, can also increase the valuation multiple through the deployment of better products and new business models and other novel and disruptive strategies (Figure 7.1).

Figure 7.1	**Digital Operating Partner Role**

- Improve sales
- Widen margins
- Lift valuation multiples

The digital operating partner is a specialist who can use digital transformation in any sector where traditional, nontechnical companies are found. Although most in private equity think IT when they hear the word *technology*, it couldn't be further from the truth, and for this reason it's useful to differentiate between technologies. Low tech, which includes IT and business systems, is somewhat commoditized and therefore not in the realm of the digital operating partner because the opportunity costs are simply too high. Same thing for mid tech, which includes automation, RPA, digital marketing and ecommerce. A good rule of thumb is if you can find a local provider to implement the tech, then it is undifferentiated, is available to any competitor and yields commensurate returns. The digital operating partner's domain is high technology, which includes the internet of things, data science (analytics and AI/ML), the digital twin, sensor fusion, additive manufacturing, AR and blockchain—tech that is highly specialized, exclusive and highly valuable.

Digital operating partners spend most of their time working outside of the buyout firm, and work in partnership with three very different groups of professionals: those responsible for investment, for management and for technology.

The digital operating partner works with the deal team throughout the life cycle of the investment. Together they work in diligence, and when an all-round strong asset is identified, they will develop the company's digital investment thesis. They continue to work together during the hold period to smooth out any bumps in the plan. And at exit, they write the language communicating the remaining digital growth opportunities.

Next the digital operating partner spends a lot of time on-site strategizing with select members of the portfolio company's management team and engineering/production. Management, and whatever internal digital team there is at kickoff, is heavily involved in shaping the digital transformation plan.

And the last group of professionals the digital operating partner works with are the techies. They are selected from the digital operating partner's proprietary partner ecosystem based on the specialized needs required to execute the bespoke digital transformation plan.

RESPONSIBILITIES

The digital operating partner is, then, part investor, part strategist and part geek. Let's look at the responsibilities that make up the job (Figure 7.2).

Identify

The digital operating partner is responsible for delivering the digital investment thesis. This investment thesis identifies the main digital themes and strategies to be deployed over the lifetime of the investment. This is the hard part and the most consequential part of the job. It can be started during

| Figure 7.2 | **Multidisciplinary Responsibilities** |

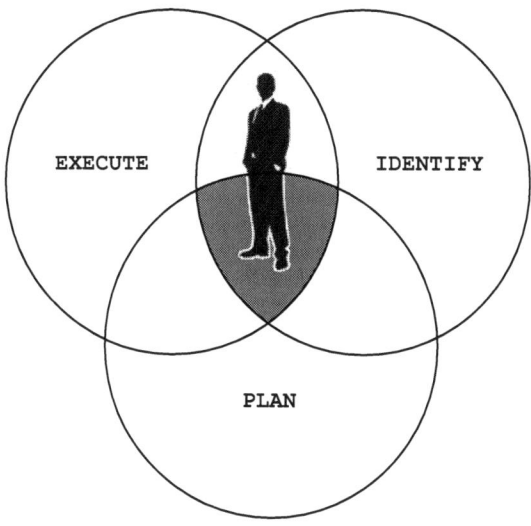

sourcing, is developed during diligence, is finalized postclosing and is revived during exit planning as part of the future growth narrative. Although each company is a snowflake, the digital operating partner applies their frameworks and detailed playbook to ensure nothing is missed and the longest digital value levers are prioritized. These value levers are stand-alone or play a supportive role to advance other themes in the investment thesis. The digital investment thesis is part of the overall investment thesis, and as such, it's incorporated into the underwriting of the transaction by the deal team. Once the transaction has closed, it provides the starting point and directional vector for the digital transformation plan.

Plan

Next in the investment sequence for the digital operating partner is developing and delivering the digital transformation plan. This can be thought of as part business plan and part requirements document. Business planning for digital includes support for the investment thesis strategies and possibly product planning, competitive analysis, resource planning and operating programs to support and package the new digital value created and the transformation process itself.

The second part of the digital transformation plan details the technical requirements for the transformation. Transformation sounds broad and expensive, but it doesn't need to be. A digital transformation simply consists of one or more digital projects to be executed. Whether this is a long list or a short list, the requirements document outlines what needs to be done.

The digital transformation plan is developed in conjunction with the portfolio company whose initial participation level is dependent on the internal digital resources available. A truncated version of the digital transformation plan is incorporated as a separate track in the 100-day plan. Besides ensuring management alignment and accountability, it includes quick wins and longer-term investments, and is used as a tool to report progress and challenges to the deal team. Its other main purpose, mostly the purpose of the requirements section, is as the input to the digital execution plan.

Execute

The next phase, which is the longest phase of the digital transformation, is getting it done: delivering the digital initiatives that when pieced together assemble into a smart feature or smart product or smart system or smart way of operating the business.

The "getting it done" part is encapsulated in the digital execution plan, and it is the responsibility of the digital operating partner to deliver a sound plan with a sound budget. Since this is a development document, the heavy lifting of producing it comes from the developers—both in-house developers, if there are any, and external developers. As a development document, it outlines in high detail the human resources, milestones, interdependencies and budget. It holds the developers, internal or external, accountable to deliver the digital transformation on spec, on time and on budget.

This highlights the importance of the digital operating partner's network. A digital transformation's probability of success is directly proportional to the talent of its developers. Talent that not only is aligned with the tasks at hand but is the best available to deliver the tasks. For this, a deep bench of third-party resources is needed. The easy way out is to throw the requirements over the fence to a known consulting firm, but that is a mistake on many levels—starting with talent and ending with budget. It's better to have an ecosystem in place consisting of a wide variety of technical service providers, vendors and subject-matter experts, who can be drawn upon differently for each digital transformation project. Each digital transformation is customized to the portfolio company's value creation needs and strategy, and as such, the external team chosen must also be customized.

But over the long term, a great external team isn't the goal. As part of the transformation, the digital operating partner also directs the buildup of an internal digital team within the portfolio company. A team to absorb the externally developed intellectual property and to carry on its development during the hold period and after the asset is sold to its next owner.

NEW AND UNIQUE

The new operating role of the digital operating partner is to create enterprise value by improving the portfolio company's EBITDA and valuation multiple, and the alpha they create is unique and invisible to the other value creation methods used today. The unique job of the digital operating partner is to lead the portfolio company through its digital transformation by guiding it through the three main steps of identifying the value, planning the value and then executing the value (Figure 7.3).

Whether the digital operating partner will be represented as an internal digital operating partner or an external fractional digital operating partner or an external digital team will depend on the PE firm, but independent of who the digital operating partner is, the digital operating partner will slot

| Figure 7.3 | Digital Operating Partner Deliverables |

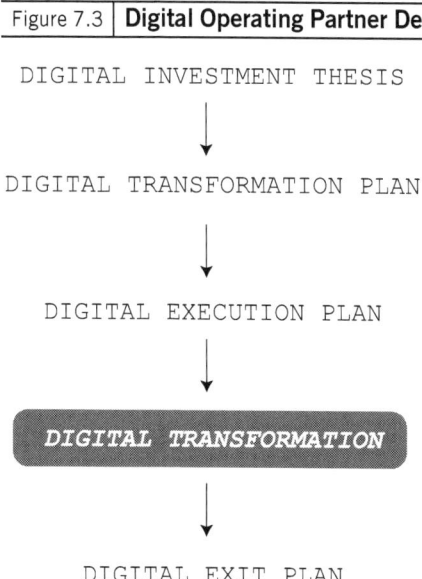

into the operations team and improve the competitiveness of both the PE firm and the firm's portfolio companies.

* * *

Now that we have a picture of this odd bird called the digital operating partner, it's time to figure out how to find one. The best way to start is to lay out the multidisciplinary and somewhat esoteric skills needed to do the job. Chapter 8 describes the ideal qualifications of the digital operating partner or digital team to successfully implement digital transformation within private equity.

CHAPTER 8

THE QUALIFICATIONS

There is a division in business today. A digital divide that separates higher-valued digital companies, which were born online and operate in bits, from lesser-valued traditional companies, which were born in the physical world and operate in atoms. Digital companies are not more valuable because they are tech companies; they are more valuable because their technological advancements have a profound effect on business. Digital changes the way we create value, what we create as value and how we monetize the value we create.

Bridging this digital divide is the digital operating partner, transforming traditional companies into digital-traditional companies. The private equity digital operating partner is a senior business executive with deep hands-on experience in strategy, technology and operations. This new PE operating role creates enterprise value for the PE's portfolio companies by developing the digital investment thesis and then realizing it with a custom digital transformation.

Because of the functional and domain breadth of the role, the digital operating partner is both highly generalized and highly specialized at the same time. Let's go through the digital operating partner's unique qualifications.

BUSINESS STRATEGY QUALIFICATIONS

Digital transformation is initiated by the digital investment thesis. This defines the strategy behind making an investment in high technology to create new intangible assets and business models. The digital investment thesis identifies the areas of incremental alpha that can be achieved by increasing sales or expanding margins or ratcheting up the valuation multiple—all forms of value creation; value from innovation and invention, value from operational efficiency and value from new business models and other novel strategies.

To select the digital initiatives that support the digital investment thesis that make up the digital transformation, not only is the digital operating partner required to be an expert in operational value creation and monetization, but because value must be prioritized in context, the digital operating partner must also be qualified to analyze industry dynamics, the competitive landscape and customer needs (Figure 8.1). The goal is to choose initiatives that create the most value and both support and advance the overall investment strategy of the portfolio company.

Figure 8.1	Business Strategy Qualifications

- Value creation and monetization
- Strategic planning
- Management

STEM QUALIFICATIONS

The digital operating partner's second area of qualifications is an all-around education in science, technology, engineering and mathematics (Figure 8.2). This is required to understand, then simulate and then innovate the value created by the smart product, service or environment.

Figure 8.2	STEM Qualifications

- Basic sciences
- Engineering
- Mathematics
- Technology
- Programming
- Data science

Digital transformation starts with understanding. Due to the wide variety of product functionality encountered, an academic background in basic science is necessary to grasp the connecting theory of the underlying physical, chemical or biological processes and their root causalities. Not understanding the theory behind the physical or chemical or biological product is folly, as this is the groundwork for every meaningful digital transformation.

To put that understanding into the context of a product requires applying the science. Applied science or engineering experience is required to appreciate the means by which the product creates value for the customer.

To quantify and then transcribe that knowledge digitally, a universal vocabulary is needed. The digital operating partner needs to not only understand the mathematics (calculus, linear algebra, differential equations) behind the engineering, but to create a digital representation of that value. The digital operating partner also needs to understand statistics, because this branch of mathematics organizes the data in a way that is consumable by data science. The most valuable intellectual property of digital transformation, and therefore of the portfolio company, is its data science models. These analytical or machine learning models are the origin of true incremental digital value.

And finally, developing data science models requires a deep and hands-on competence in technology. Not low tech, like IT and business systems. And not mid tech, like RPA, automation, digital marketing and ecommerce. But high technology like the internet of things, data science (analytics and AI/ML), the digital twin, sensor fusion, additive manufacturing, AR and blockchain, because these are the tech building blocks of any digital transformation.

Gluing everything together is computer science. The digital operating partner should know how to program—to understand in a practical way how science, engineering, mathematics and technology are pulled together and productized.

OPERATIONAL QUALIFICATIONS

Once the digital investment thesis is approved and a custom digital transformation plan is designed, both need to be brought into existence by good ol'-fashioned hands-on execution. This is the third area of qualifications required from the digital operating partner (Figure 8.3).

A digital transformation, like every other business transformation, consists of many small steps. To execute these small steps, in this case, to execute the digital initiatives, requires both hard and soft skills.

Figure 8.3	Operational Qualifications

- Project management
- Commercialization
- Hiring external digital teams from large network of technical service providers
- Building internal digital teams
- CEO coaching
- Been there, done that credibility

Hard skills here are the skills needed to deliver a software or data science project on spec, on time and on budget. This comes from experience in developing and delivering commercial digital products. Successfully delivering a digital transformation means hiring external digital teams and building internal digital teams. External teams are hired to quickly build critical mass and onboard the experience needed to get the project started. To be effective the digital operating partner will have a deep and proprietary ecosystem of technical vendors, service providers and subject-matter experts to choose from.

Developing a smart feature or a smart product or a smart service as part of a digital transformation is a technical challenge for sure, but developing any of them within a traditional company, with its unique culture and all its human idiosyncrasies, is a completely different challenge that requires softer skills. Although it's easier to do this within a buyout-owned portfolio company (see Chapter 7), it is nevertheless challenging and essential to get right. These skills all start with credibility.

Digital transformations are not managed; they are led. To be effective, the digital operating partner must gain the trust of the CEO and prove the value of the digital operating partner to the entire management team. The digital operating partner must have the business acumen, credibility and empathy essential to coach the CEO and be approachable enough to have domain-specific conversations with everyone from the functional group heads down to the specialized scientists, engineers and tradespeople. This comes from having done it all before: experience in leading a company or P&L and experience in delivering technical projects to commercialization are crucial qualifications. Not from a consulting perspective, but from the view of authoritative operating experience within an enterprise.

WIDE AND DEEP

The ideal digital operating partner is an interdisciplinary in business strategy, in science and technology and in operations (Figure 8.4). The ideal digital operating partner needs a wide enough and deep enough body of education and experience to make the right choices when creating the digital investment thesis, developing the digital transformation plan and then executing it. This is to have a knowledge canvas large enough to see patterns and connect the dots between disciplines to deliver outsized enterprise value.

Figure 8.4 | Multidisciplinary Qualifications

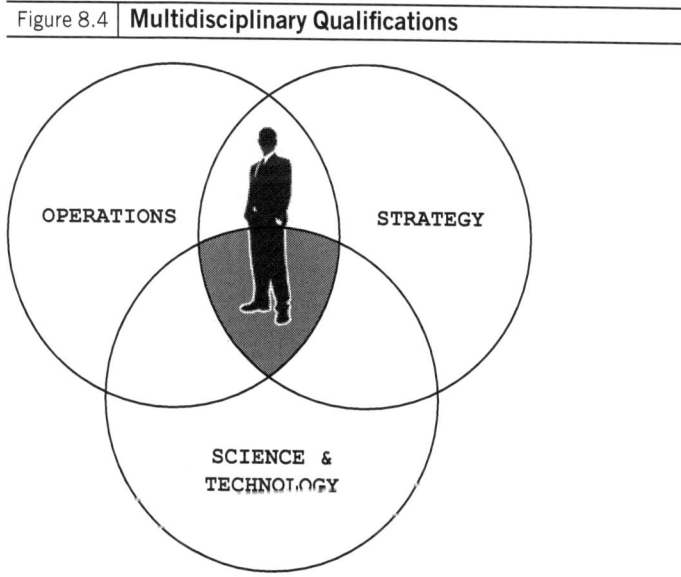

CONCLUSION

BRING IT ON!

I had just landed in Grand Rapids to meet a client the next day and was making my way to ground transportation while searching my phone for my hotel's address. I didn't have a car lined up, so I was getting an Uber. As I walked outside, the app told me it was going to be a 20-minute wait. 20 minutes!

As I looked up from my phone, right in front of me was a line of taxis with no one waiting. 20 minutes, damn. I never take taxis, but a 20-minute wait was unbearable, so I poked my head in the first taxi's passenger window and asked, "How much?" It wasn't a fixed rate, but since the price of the driver's initial estimate would be less than half the cost of my Uber, I hopped in against my better judgment.

Yep, just like I remembered: crappy car, knees pushed up against some protective device and a commercial for a late-night talk show blaring in my face. Great.

Then it began. After I gave him the exact address, the meter didn't go on, and when I inquired why, I was informed that for that location, at that time of the day, there was a surcharge, and it would be extra for my carry-on sitting beside me, and . . . I didn't let him finish his arithmetic. I knew a bad thing when I saw it, so I asked him to stop and let me out. Desperate to keep the fare he waited two hours for, he kept on rolling. I had to get out of this torture chamber, so I opened the back door as the car was slowing down to merge into traffic and jumped out into traffic with bag in tow and no sidewalk in sight.

Think about that. The customer experience was so bad that I was willing to risk my safety to wait another 20 minutes for a 30-minute ride. Although extreme, that's the difference between a smart product and a traditional product, and that's the opportunity we have in front of us today for every kind of traditional product. Smart is so much better.

The good news for cab companies is technology has matured since Uber built its custom platform and app. A vast majority of what Uber custom-coded is now available off the shelf, available to taxi companies and any other companies that want to "Uberize" their business model.

A WAVE IS COMING

A wave of technology, led by digital transformation, is washing over all traditional sectors. Digital transformation, through the internet of things, is an extension of the internet into machines and equipment, enabling companies to gather and use their data to make smart machines and smart equipment. This smart megatrend, which increases the intangible asset share of enterprise value, is now ready to be capitalized on by private equity investors.

BRINGING IT ALL TOGETHER

A successful digital transformation is part finding the right digital initiatives, part finding the right portfolio company and part finding the right digital operating partner, corresponding, respectively, to Parts One, Two and Three of this book. The digital operating partner and their extended team identify, plan and execute valuable digital initiatives to transform traditional companies into data-driven companies with more innovative products, business models and operations. And that's about it. When distilled, the main takeaway from this book is, *digital transformation is a new and powerful value creation tool that's most effectively applied to traditional/legacy portfolio companies by the private equity digital operating partner.*

DIGITAL TRANSFORMATION IS THE NEWEST VALUE CREATION TOOL

Digital transformation is an untapped value creation tool whose tech has matured out of venture to become the newest tool for private equity.

It increases enterprise value by increasing both EBITDA and the valuation multiple. Revenue is grown by increasing market share through innovation and by increasing TAM through product invention. Profit margins are expanded by reducing COGS and OPEX through operational efficiency. The valuation multiple is increased by supporting the primary investment thesis and through the so-called digital rerate. The digital rerate lifts the valuation multiple toward tech valuation multiples, through innovative business models and other novel strategies, accounted for on the acquiring company's balance sheet as goodwill. While most other value creation levers are capped by modest percentage improvements in cost savings, the ceiling of digital transformation is high. High because its main focus is to improve revenue and the way portfolio companies do business.

As a wealth-generation platform, it keeps on giving, by making secondary buyouts possible on both ends of the hold period. Since digital transformation is independent of traditional value creation techniques, it can make a good sponsor-owned company better, and since a digital transformation is never done, it points to a path of more value creation for the next buyer.

TRADITIONAL COMPANIES ARE THE BEST FIT

LBOs and their portfolio companies provide the best conditions for digital transformation success. The active management style of private equity is made for change, which is needed for any operational transformation, including digital transformation. Traditional/legacy, or nontech, portfolio companies make up a majority of private equity's inventory, and since they are traditional companies, and by definition not tech companies, they have the most to gain from digital transformation. Once transformed into data-driven companies, traditional companies are anointed with the same "superpowers" used by the most valuable tech companies. Superpowers that enable new ways for traditional companies to grow. Superpowers that enable new business models and create intangible assets. Digital transformation gives traditional companies an edge over their competitors and indirectly provides their owners with an edge. An edge that results in more outsized returns than would otherwise be possible.

THE DIGITAL OPERATING PARTNER MAKES IT HAPPEN

The role of the digital operating partner is the same as the role of other operating partners: to increase enterprise value. While the role is the same, the responsibilities differ greatly. The digital operating partner is responsible for leading select portfolio companies through their digital transformation journey. To do this, the digital operating partner is involved in every stage of the deal, from doing diligence, to identifying, planning and executing digital initiatives, to developing a digital growth narrative at exit. The digital operating partner creates operational and strategic improvements by delivering on the digital investment thesis, digital transformation plan and digital execution plan.

For the cab company or any other company that wants to Uberize its business model, the digital operating partner would bring in the right teams of experts in the internet of things for telematics and machine learning for scheduling to build an aggregator platform with mostly off-the-shelf components.

To do this the digital operating partner must be interdisciplinary—qualified in business strategy, in science and technology and in operations—to get things done. This manifests itself into a job that is full-time or fractional, internal or external, individual or team oriented.

WHAT'S NEXT

As you've been reading this book, a few portfolio companies have probably come to mind that could benefit from being digitally transformed. Or maybe you just read a CIM that completely missed digital as a growth opportunity. In any case, the next step is to socialize digital transformation as a value creation tool within your firm. If in agreement, then identify an existing or new portfolio company or other target that seems to fit the criteria for digital transformation success. The best practice is to make digital transformation part of the original investment thesis, but there are plenty of corner cases that can also yield great returns. If you find a good fit, bring in a digital operating partner to begin a new value creation journey.

If you resonated with this book and want to dig deeper, I have a few more resources for you. My first book, *IoT Inc*,

CONCLUSION

will go deeper and wider into the tech, business and strategy of digital transformation. To get techy, pick through over 100 episodes of my podcast that can be found on Spotify, iTunes and other podcast platforms. Finally, to learn more about what a digital operating partner can do for your firm and your portfolio companies, check out digitaloperatingpartners.com.

INDEX

Page numbers followed by *f* refer to figures.

Additive manufacturing, 44–45
Advertising industry, 36
AI, 43
Airline industry, 21
Alpha, digital transformation
    creating, 14, 37–38, 38*f*
Alphabet, 27, 28, 36
Amazon:
    and benefits of being digital, 12
    competitive advantage of, 3, 5, 7, 63, 64
    data-driven products from, 65
Analytics, 43
Antitrust, 63
Anything as a service (XaaS) model, 21
Apple, 27–29, 36
Apple Music, 29, 36
AR (augmented reality), 45
Assets growth profile, 33, 33*f*
Augmented reality (AR), 45

Auto insurance, 7
Autoclave, 18–19, 19*f*
Automation, 31, 41–42
Autopilot, 7

Best practices, 15–24, 98
    business model innovation and invention, 20–22
    digital transformation as value creation tool, 23–24
    operational efficiency improvements, 22–23
    product innovation, 17–18
    product invention, 18–20
Biotech, 22
Blockchain, 45
Business model innovation and invention, 20–22
Business strategy qualifications, 86–87, 87*f*
Business systems, 10, 40–41
Buyout firms, 32, 58, 77

101

INDEX

Cash flow:
    data-driven operational
        improvements
        increasing, 26
    increasing, with digital
        transformation, 12
CEOs, 57, 90
COGS:
    about, 31, 32f
    lowering, 76
    operational efficiency
        lowering, 22
    reducing, 96
Company life cycle, 49
Company ownership
    structures, 53–61, 59f
    as competitive advantage,
        59–60
    corporate vs. portfolio,
        56–57
    digital transformation
        across different, 60–61
    public vs. private, 54–56
    venture vs. buyout, 58–59
Computer science, 89
Continental Tire, 29–30
Corporate companies,
    portfolio vs., 56–57
Cost cutting, 22
C-suite, 57
Customer(s):
    collecting data about (see
        Customer data)
    connection to, in digital
        companies, 6
Customer data:
    in digital-traditional
        companies, 11
    importance of, 6–7
    and OPEX, 31–32
    power of, 63–64
    for product innovation, 17
    and revenue, 28
    for smart products, 65

Data, customer (see Customer
    data)
Data science, 10, 22, 43–44,
    88
Data-driven companies:
    competitive advantage of,
        63–66, 66f, 97
    digital transformation
        producing, 13, 16
    innovation in, 3
    transformation to, 13–14
Deliverables, 83f
Developers, 81
Digital:
    benefits of being, 12–13
    competitive advantage of
        being, 64–66
Digital companies:
    defined, 4, 6f
    traditional vs., 6–9, 11
Digital diligence, 70, 70f
Digital divide, 85
Digital goodwill, 12, 35, 37f
Digital investment thesis,
    78–79, 86 (See also
    Investment thesis
    support)
Digital marketing, 42
Digital operating partner:
    about, 73
    defined, xviii
    deliverables, 83f
    enterprise value created by,
        82–83
    qualifications of (see
        Qualifications)
    responsibilities of, 78–82,

INDEX

79*f*
role of, 9, 15–16, 76–78, 76*f*, 97
Digital payoff, 37–38
Digital rerate, 34–37, 37*f*, 96
Digital team, internal, 82
Digital transformation:
  about, 1
  company traits for, 66–67
  defined, 9–10, 9*f*, 16, 75–76
  execution phase for, 81–82, 89
  and high technology, 3
  identify phase of, 78–79
  planning phase for, 80
  in private vs. public companies, 55
  success factors for, 61*f*
  value creation from, 95–96
  as value creation tool, 23–24
Digital twin, 44
Digital-traditional companies:
  competitive advantage of, when data-driven, 64–65
  defined, 11
  traditional vs. digital vs., 11*f*
Diligence, 70, 70*f*, 77
Disruption, 35–36, 37*f*
Distributed ledger technology (DLT), 45
Distribution, direct, 7

Early-stage companies, 47
EBITDA, 27, 76, 82
Ecommerce, 42
Engineering/production, 78, 88

Enterprise value, increasing, 26–27, 95–96
Execution, 81–82

Facebook, 63
Financial metrics, 25–38
  digital payoff, 37–38
  digital rerate, 34–37
  EBITDA, 27
  enterprise value, 26–27
  investment thesis support, 33
  market share, 28–29
  market size, 29–30
  profit margin, 30–32
  revenue, 27–28
  valuation multiple, 32
Ford, 8
Full digital stack, 48, 49*f*

GE (General Electric), 21, 36
General Motors (GM), 7, 8
Goodwill, 12, 35, 37*f*, 96
Google, 36, 63
Google Ads, 36
Governance, 54

Hardware-defined products, 43
High technology:
  about, 43–46
  and company maturity, 68
  for data-driven companies, 13–14
  digital synonymous with, 1
  for digital transformation, 10
  and digitalization level, 68
  impact of, 40*f*
  for mature companies, 48
  and role of digital operating partner, 77, 88

Industrial internet of things (IIoT), 31
Industrie 4.0 (I40), 31
Initiative, choosing, 9, 86
Innovation, 3, 63, 96
Innovative business models, 35–36
Internal digital team, 82
Internet of things (IoT), 10, 43
Investment thesis support, 33, 33*f*, 78–79
IoT (internet of things), 10, 43
IoT, Inc (Sinclair), 98–99
IT, 40, 77
ITunes, 28–29, 36

John Deere, 29, 36

LBO capital portfolio companies:
 as best fit for digital transformation, 96–97
 competitive advantage of, 60
 venture vs., 58–59
Leadership:
 effective, 54–55
 importance of support from, 57
Life cycle, company, 49
Logistics, 22
Long-term trends, 15
Low technology:
 about, 40–41
 and company maturity, 68
 and digital transformation, 10
 for early-stage companies, 47
 impact of, 40*f*
 and role of digital operating partner, 77

Machine learning, 43–44
Management team, 78
Manufacturing, additive, 44–45
Market(s):
 legacy, 69
 nondisrupted, 69
 share of, 13, 28–29
 size of, 13, 29–30
Marketing, digital, 42
Mathematics, 88
Mature companies, 48, 68–69
Maturity, technical, 68
Metrics, financial (*see* Financial metrics)
Microsoft, 27–29, 36
Mid technology:
 about, 41–43
 and company maturity, 68
 and digital transformation, 10
 impact of, 40*f*
 for mid-stage companies, 47–48
 and role of digital operating partner, 77
Mid-stage companies, 47–48
Monetizability models, 20–21
Music industry, 36

Networking tech, 28
Nondisrupted markets, 69
Non-sponsor-owned companies, 56–57

Operating model, 59
Operational efficiency:
 automation for, 42

INDEX

and customer data, 7
digital transformation
  increasing, 96
  improvements in, 22–23
Operational improvements:
  and enterprise value, 26
  and revenue, 27
Operational qualifications,
  89–91, 89f
OPEX:
  about, 31–32, 32f
  lowering, 76, 96
  operational efficiency
    lowering, 22
Ownership:
  percentage of, 58
  structures of company (see
    Company ownership
    structures)

Payoff, digital, 37–38
Planning, 80
Portfolio companies:
  as best fit for digital
    transformation, 96–97
  best suited for digital
    transformation, 70
"Power by the hour" business
  model, 21
Prediction models, 19–20
Pricing, 20–21
Privacy, 11
Private companies, public vs.,
  54–56
Private equity, value of digital
  transformation in, 16
Product(s):
  data-driven, 65
  defined, xviii
  hardware-defined, 43
  innovation in, 17–18

invention of, 18–20
smart, 65–66, 90
software defined, 43
technology as, in digital
  companies, 5
traditional, 4
Profit margin, 30–32
Public companies, private vs.,
  54–56

Qualifications, 85–91
  business strategy, 86–87,
    87f
  operational, 89–91, 89f
  STEM, 87–89, 87f

Reporting, quarterly, 55
Rerate, digital, 34–37, 37f, 96
Revenue, 27–28, 30f
Revenue model, 8
Road roller, 17–18, 18f
Robotaxi, 8, 36
Robotic process automation
  (RPA), 41–42
Robots, 31
Rolls Royce, 21
RPA (robotic process
  automation), 41–42

Sales, 12, 76
Science, 88, 89
Self-driving models, 7
Sensor fusion, 44
SG&A spending, 32
Siddeley, Bristol, 21
Skills, hand, 89–90
Smart products, 65–66, 90
Software defined products, 43
Sponsor-owned portfolio
  companies, 56–57
Steam roller, 17–18, 18f

STEM qualifications, 87–89, 87*f*
Supply chain, visibility of, 22

Technical maturity, 68
Technical requirements, for transformation, 80
Technology, 39–50
  classified by impact, 40*f*
  competency in, 88
  deciding when to apply which, 46–49, 47*f*
  and digital, 39
  for digital products, 10
  distributed ledger, 45
  high (*see* High technology)
  and IT, 77
  and life cycle impact, 49–50
  low (*see* Low technology)
  mid (*see* Mid technology)
  networking, 28
  new wave of, 94–95
  value added with, 76
Tesla:
  and benefits of being digital, 12
  competitive advantage of, 3, 5, 7, 64
  data-driven products from, 65
  digital innovation at, 8
  innovative business model of, 36
  products and offerings, 7–8

3D printing, 44–45
Toyota, 8
Traditional companies:
  as best fit for digital transformation, 96–97
  defined, 4, 5*f*
  digital vs., 6–9, 11
  traits of, for potential digital transformation, 67–68
Traditional products, 4
Transformation plan, 80

Uber:
  and benefits of being digital, 12
  competitive advantage of, 3, 5, 7, 26, 64
  data-driven products from, 65
Usability models, 17, 18*f*
Utility models, 18–19, 19*f*

Valuation migration, 34–35, 34*f*, 37*f*
Valuation multiple, 12, 32, 82
Venture capital portfolio companies, 58–59
Virtual reality (VR), 45

Windows, 29

XaaS (anything as a service) model, 21
Xbox game console, 29

ABOUT THE AUTHOR

Bruce Sinclair is a business consultant whose 30-year career has encompassed high technology, business and investment. He began as a mathematician and then programmer who quickly found his way to business through marketing. He worked his way through product marketing and brand management to be VP of Marketing for a large Microsoft subsidiary. After that, he was the CEO of a number of software companies before moving into consulting.

Bruce wrote the bestselling digital transformation book, *IoT Inc*, published by McGraw-Hill in 2017, and has certified hundreds of professionals with his ICIP program and thousands more with his courses on LinkedIn Learning.

Since 2015, Bruce has focused his experience on advising companies on how to use digital transformation to create enterprise value—first as an independent consultant and then as an operating partner for a middle-market private equity firm with $1.5 billion in committed capital.

Find out more at digitaloperatingpartners.com and iot-inc.com.

Printed in Great Britain
by Amazon